Blimey!
Another Book About London

Blimey!
Another Book About London

by
DONALD GODDARD

 QUADRANGLE BOOKS

A New York Times Company

Contents

Foreword

*J*UST the titles of books about London fill three whole volumes of the British Museum Library catalogue, so who needs another one?

Anybody who doesn't know London well, or at all, and who wants to engage with that seductive, bewildering city in a rather more intimate way than through the tinted windows of an air-conditioned cattle truck—that's who needs it. If they can't have a Londoner to guide them, they can at least have a Londoner's book.

The first half should give them an idea of what to expect. Too many tourists, taken by surprise, waste far too much time just boggling at London's improbable bulk and variety. It should also help them understand what kind of people live there, not least because of Barney Bosshart's marvelous pictures, which catch their temper and spirit far better than I could describe them.

The rest of the book then proposes a number of quite arbitrary ways of cutting the city down to size and creaming off the best of everything. After they've been there awhile, visitors will no doubt start finding places and things they like even better, but this way they won't waste a minute.

All the practical stuff, the sifted-out names, addresses and phone numbers, are listed in the back. If there are any complaints, I'll be glad to pass them on to Lisa Kyle, who ruined her social life doing the research, and Theresa Davis, who ruined her eyesight typing the manuscript.

And they, in turn, will probably blame Natalie Donay Goddard, American exile, because it was she who made this book happen—like everything else.

D.G.

February, 1972

Section I

Chapter One
London is . . .

*L*ONDON *is.* She's not to be argued with. Like nature in another aspect, she exists to some inscrutable purpose of her own, indifferent to our pain or pleasure.

London is 2,000 years old. Begun by the Romans, she endured the dark ages, the Norman conquest, the Great Plague and the Great Fire. She survived the speculative builder, the slum-clearance schemes of the German Luftwaffe and the first bombardment in history by ballistic missile. All sorts and conditions of men have left their mark on her, not just in stone but in custom, tradition and manners that are not to be questioned, any more than one would question the natural order of the seasons. For four hundred years, she shaped the world, and did so with a sense of fitness.

London is bricks and mortar, but is not to be understood in that light, as 700 square miles of urban sprawl speckled with ancient glories. To move on with no more to show for a visit than a few feet of exposed Kodachrome and a sweater from Marks & Spencer's is like leaving a strip joint thinking you understand women.

London is a fine spring morning, early, in Hyde Park. Tit-tupping horses on Rotten Row snort skittish breaths of steam. Kensington ladies and gentlemen, collars turned up against the cold, call sharply to their dogs, who scud about half-crazed with smells and freedom, raising pigeons. Trees misted with green growth etch their upper works against an unlikely sky of gold and heraldic blue. Rugs of crocus splash purple and yellow on the grass. And gulls by the hundred wheel and quarrel over the black waters of the Serpentine, obscur-

3

ing the groundbase of traffic till themselves overborne by a 747 on its final approach to Heathrow.

London is Leather Lane at lunchtime, an everyday market for everyday people, with nothing for tourists to buy—unless they fancy a can of hairspray or a package of cut-price razor blades. The ordinary life of London surfaces here, without pomp, without glamour, but not without style. In this nondescript street, marked at the Holborn end by the Prudential's red Gothic cathedral to the greater glory of life insurance and flanked on the east by the diamond deposits of Hatton Garden, working-class shoppers gather each day to skirmish with the cost of living.

When money is tight, stores can be inhibiting. Pennywatchers risk the scorn of clerks no better off than they are. But down the Lane it's different. They're on their own ground, among their own kind, and all they have to worry about when buying a pound of tomatoes is that the man gives them the firm ones from the front of the barrow and not the bruised ones at the back.

And not just tomatoes. Fruit and meat and packaged groceries. Sweaters and socks and bicycle tires. Cut flowers, candy and carpet slippers. A man selling linens threatens a group of skeptical mums with a pair of cellophane-wrapped sheets, horribly checked in pink, green and blue: "Right, then. Pay attention. Look here—the last pair. I'm really having a go this time. Am I asking two pound? No. Thirty bob, then? No. Here, come on, somebody—give me a pound. Just to clear 'em out of the way."

So confident is he of making a sale, he's already picking out the next item, a flaring red bath towel with appliqué daisies. Nobody moves. "What?" He can't believe it. "A quid? For a pair of sheets?" He must be losing his mind. "Come on, darlings—have a go. Spend the rent. Do something drastic." They won't. "No?" No. "Nobody?" Nobody. He sighs, and whacks the sheets into his partner's middle. "Right, then. Put 'em back in the safe, Charlie."

And so it goes on. Panty hose, saucepans and paint. Suitcases, records and shaving cream. A sale here, a joke there. It's a scaled-down Petticoat Lane, without the tourists and self-conscious slummers who have nothing better to do of a Sunday morning than visit a human zoo. This is one of many London markets where working-class people side-step a middle-class economy to score a point or two.

London is the cry of the trendy on the Fulham Road. In the Sixties, a handful of talented people in pop music, fashion and films won for the city a mercifully brief moment of glory as a mecca for swingers. And although that bubble soon burst, Carnaby Street, the King's Road and Kensington High Street are still overrun by apers of their life-style and by the wheeler-dealers who cater to it. Fulham Road is where *Vogue*'s beautiful people often eat, and so that's where trendies eat, too, assembling there most evenings in their orange Porsches, red Alfas, green Lotuses, purple beach buggies and decal-plastered Minis to graze in flocks on scallopine at San Frediano or on hamburgers at The Great American Disaster and to price each other's gear.

This is the new aristocracy, born of glamour industries and purchasing power—TV and advertising people, models and PR girls, photographers, designers and boutique proprietors. They are the mercenary soldiers of the class war, drawn from both sides of the tracks and owing allegiance to the highest bidder. For them, social status depends on being first with the latest, whatever it may be, and so they watch each other closely. This explains why they walk into you on the street and drive dented automobiles.

There is the noisy "up" trendy, secure in his garment labels, loudly in love with himself and the moment, and the sullen "down" trendy, bored and spiteful—so what can life do for me next? To see them at play can be amusing—now and again—but overexposure has been known to put some people off perfectly good restaurants for life and to convert others into blood-lusting revolutionaries.

Those who find conspicuous consumption offensive tend to dine early in Chelsea, Knightsbridge and Kensington.

London is arrogant. Where New Yorkers derive a certain melancholy satisfaction from visitors picking their city to pieces, accepting this as an implied tribute to their sharpness and fortitude, Londoners often turn haughty. Let a tourist complain about pub-licensing hours or criticize the 73-bus service or otherwise suggest any unfavorable comparison between London and his hometown and he will either be patted tolerantly on the head or given the impression that he ought to go back there.

It's not really a matter of local pride; Londoners grouse all the time. They don't think London is perfect—just better than anywhere else. Indeed, encountered in its most extreme form, this impregnable self-esteem can actually make London's shortcomings seem more worthy than other cities' accomplishments. Outside criticism is simply not relevant.

This can be very irritating. The implication is that strangers are too coarse-grained to appreciate the subtler virtues of London life. And even when a Londoner *can* be persuaded to acknowledge, say, the greater convenience of a public transportation system that runs all night, like New York's, as compared with one that closes down around midnight, like London's, he will manage to do so in a way which plainly suggests that the advantage is of little or no consequence anyway.

What is even more maddening, he tends to treat praise of London in much the same spirit. How can a foreigner possibly comprehend her true quality when he lacks that finer edge of discrimination which only London can impart? He'll accept the compliment graciously and change the subject or pass it off as a joke.

The fact is, the Londoner doesn't *care* what you think.

His city was built to rule the world, and so she did for a time, with one foot in Asia, the other in Africa, and both hands busy in people's pockets from Hudson Bay to the Tasman Sea. But now history has made her a basket case, lopping off the limbs of empire. What's left is the trunk, powerful yet impotent, full of organs too grand and imposing to be entirely suited to her reduced circumstances yet still providing a wonderfully rich and varied texture to life for those who can afford it, shot through with pleasing inefficiencies and luxuries of spirit.

The change has come quickly, too quickly for many to grasp. Indeed, Londoners born before the second German war probably never will understand what has happened. And this vanished authority has left in its after-glow a faintly bewildered air. The city still supports all the trappings of a great imperial capital, but the clatter of cavalry in the streets is pure theater now, awakening no ominous echoes in India or the Sudan. And the elaborate ceremonial of a state opening of Parliament is quite disproportionate to the real importance of a government in pawn to political and economic interests centered elsewhere. But there is no sense of play-acting. Pageantry and ritual still feel like the working out of natural law. London simply cannot bring herself to distinguish between the symbols of power and its reality. The panoply and institutions are still there; so is the cast of mind.

Four centuries of dominion over absurdly large tracts of territory and over foreign peoples outnumbering her own population a hundred times or more have bred self-assurance in the bone. London is, for the most part, a calm, unassertive city, assuming a pre-eminence in human affairs without thought or question. Her citizens will take a polite interest in the way others behave, but having always taught the rest of the world how to do things, feel they have nothing to learn. It is a conviction which lies beyond the reach of serious doubt; being so unshakably *right*, they can afford to allow others to think as they wish and to live as they choose. Thus is London's much advertised tolerance of eccentrics, fanatics, cranks and rebels not so much a virtue as the ultimate vanity.

London is lazy, though some call it relaxed. She'll organize brilliantly, incomparably, in times of emergency; with the ordinary business of living she tends to muddle along, slow-footed, quick-witted, with much in reserve. Honest in large things, undependable in small. Unless the Londoner likes the look of you or is deeply involved in his work, almost anything can prove too much trouble. Shop assistants, for example, often prefer to weave little fancies about the non-delivery of left-handed niblicks rather than look in the stockroom. They'll be very nice about it, however. They may even direct you miles across town to their nearest competitor, who won't have them either (or else won't admit it).

As against that, try fainting on the street. Where New Yorkers would probably step over you and Parisians step *on* you, Londoners will cluck and fuss and produce cups of tea till the ambulance comes. Their concern is quite genuine but also self-serving. Any excuse will do to break the rhythm of work, which may be why 60,000 refugees from the American way of urban life have settled down here and stopped biting their cuticles. Londoners admire affluence, in a curiously un-envious way, and respect the magic of money like everyone else—but not enough to keep their stores open late or to take work home on weekends. In London, only the trains run on time.

London is shadowed by a development plan. This may not be as ominous as it sounds—*un*planned development is prob-ably the worst thing that can happen to a modern city—but it's ominous enough in an age which has reduced architecture to a branch of cost accountancy. The London Hilton was planned, that grubby reminiscence of Miami Beach peeking over the Queen's garden wall. And so was the Shell Center across the river from Whitehall, a lumpish celebration of oil company profits walling in the south bank with all the grace and style of Sing Sing. This century has not dealt kindly with London. It began with a cancerous spread of vile suburbs eating into the countryside like ink through blotting paper, and it looks as though it may end with arrows of high-speed motorway piercing her through the heart.

And yet in some ways, London probably stands a better chance of survival as a place fit to live in than any of the other great capitals. Where else is the air getting purer and the rivers cleaner? What other city of anything like her size can point to a steady *rise* in sunshine hours and the return of birds and flowers which haven't been seen there for 150 years? Planners must take some credit for that.

Then, too, the motorist, the commuter, the tourist and real-estate developer—those four horsemen of the urban apo-calypse—meet their sternest resistance here, again thanks in part to the planner. By pulling the strands of danger together, he not only brings it into sharper focus but embodies it in his person. If those Londoners who still care about such things were required to contend piecemeal with every new threat that arose, they would very soon cease to care. Defense of the old order would be as futile as taking a baseball bat to a plague of locusts. But when the planners must make a public pitch for every project seriously affecting the character and quality of London life, there is at least some point in going to the plate. The conservationists will strike out as often as not, of course, but one hit can reprieve a whole neighborhood.

Yet if planners are better than no planners, they are still not to be trusted. The Greater London Development Plan shows a proper regard for civilized values, but also reflects a disquieting preoccupation with growth projections for car ownership and tourism. Planners see themselves as the servants of "progress," not its masters. They have left it to others to decide whether, for instance, civilization and the private automobile are compatible in cities.

If the American experience is any guide, the Parkinson's Law of Road-Building is that traffic expands to take up the space made available, and even a modest attempt to adapt London to the motorist, as foreshadowed in the plan, will entail knocking down—in the middle of a crippling housing shortage—at least 25,000 homes, not all of them marvels of domestic architecture, to be sure, but probably pleasanter to look at than anything likely to replace them. And once the principle of traffic priority is conceded, the logic of further "progress" becomes irresistible. If you can cut a swath through Kensington, Earls Court and Chelsea—as the Greater London Council fully intends to do—then why not another through Belgravia, Mayfair and Westminster? There will be nothing to stop London going the way of Los Angeles.

Similarly with hotels. The number of visitors to London has topped eight million a year; there *is* a shortage of bedrooms. But if development continues in the next decade at the same rate as it did in the last, there may be nothing much left for hotel guests to admire in central London but other hotels. Or pudding-faced buildings that *look* like hotels. And at that point, they will presumably stop coming.

True, the city is big enough to take a lot of punishment, but the construction cranes have been pecking at her carcass now for 20 years. And as the possible disadvantage of destroying the very qualities that bring people to London in order to accommodate them once they get here doesn't seem to have dawned on the planners yet, the worst may still be to come—although that hardly seems possible after the Churchill Hotel in Portman Square.

———————

London is . . .

. . . "please" and "thank you" and "luv" and "ducky" and

five skinheads beating up a Pakistani bus conductor on Stepney High Street . . .

. . . a morning army of grim-faced commuters marching 10-deep, 30,000 an hour, across London Bridge into a deserted financial district and marching out as grimly again at night . . .

. . . hand-lettered postcards, with telephone numbers, displayed in candy-store windows: FRENCH LADY SEEKS INTERESTING POSITION. SWEDISH GOVERNESS, EXPERT WITH STOCKS AND BONDS . . .

. . . an elderly scholar in the murmurous hush of the British Museum's Reading Room, nodding over his books at G7, the seat where Marx wrote "Das Kapital" . . .

. . . church bells calling out a handful of the faithful in the dusk of a still Sunday evening, spires and belfries blackening against a green sky . . .

. . . hairy poets haggardly sipping Chilean Cabernet in Bernard Stone's Turret Bookshop . . .

. . . football match yobboes slashing the seats of an Underground train . . .

. . . a legal abortion . . .

. . . tea at the Ritz . . .

. . . feeding the ducks . . .

London is anything a lively mind would have her be. Whatever is expected of a great city can be found here, good and bad alike, but often only by those prepared to seek it out. Casual travelers will probably have a better time in Paris or Rome or Venice, for the virtue of those places is more accessible to the passive eye.

London is the compendium of urban experience. She lends balance and perspective to her citizens' affairs, tempering the ambitious, encouraging the curious and, in her infinite diversity, denying hardly anyone the consolations of hope.

Chapter Two

... matter of fact

*P*EOPLE once gathered in cities for safety, convenience and comfort; now they are abandoning them for the same reasons. Every year, those moving out of London exceed the number moving in by 90,000. By 1981, the city's population should be down to around 7 million, which may please the planners but is of small consolation to the homeward-bound office worker who suspects that most of those left will still be using Oxford Street tube station between 5 and 6.

City dwellers are, by nature, grumblers—and not without reason. The story of urban life is one long, impossible struggle to organize an environment that will reconcile the conflicting needs, interests and esthetic preferences of large numbers of people who are either unwilling or unable to pay the bills. Noise, dirt, slums and inadequate services are products of congestion—which is simply another word for the urban condition. And since all a city government has ever been able to do is mitigate its consequences, the only question is, how much congestion can people take?

In London, as in most other cities, the middle class is answering with its feet. But the message may never come through as loud and as clear as it has in New York, for instance, because London enjoys a special advantage. Where New York, like Paris, is solid and concentrated, London is diffuse and multi-cellular. Instead of just spreading outwards from a center core into vacant country, she began as twins, merged together and grew by mopping up a daisy chain of satellite towns and villages that still preserve some sense of identity. This is one of the keys to London. Hampstead, Highgate and Camden Town; Fulham and Chelsea; Islington, Hackney, Clapham, Dulwich and Camberwell—there are scores of them—all had

11

lives of their own long before the lava flow of Victorian villas silted in the gaps and rolled on relentlessly into Edwardian and more recent wastes of suburbia. And some of that life still remains. There's still something individual in most of them, some faint but discernible difference in character and atmosphere. It's one of the city's subtler charms.

Indeed, even in central London, it is still possible to step out of the crowd, turn a couple of corners and be alone on the sidewalk. The city's pressure points are usually padded with softer tissue. In the parks and squares and the maze of streets are endless changes of mood and pace. There's still room to breathe and move about.

Exactly how much room is hard to say. The Corporation of the City of London may be strictly correct when it insists on 677 acres—the bit the Romans built a wall around, plus as much again outside—but the 610 *square miles* administered by the Greater London Council is more realistic. But then what about the 235 square miles of the London postal area? Or the 786 square miles of the Metropolitan Police district? Or the 900-odd square miles served by the main network of London Transport?

These territories are administrative accidents—arbitrary history rather than rational geography. The city is roughly 30 miles wide by 25 miles across, and seems twice that, at least, from behind the wheel of a car trying to get in or get out on a summer weekend.

London's special problem, and special attraction, is that she's a national capital, a major seaport, a hub of international trade and finance, an industrial complex, a cultural and communications center, a tourist mecca and a historical monument all rolled up into one. The city is so big, in fact, that she should be unmanageable, but in practice works amazingly well, considering that 34 independently elected local government bodies share the responsibility—with the help of two police departments, four electricity boards, three gas boards, four metropolitan regional hospital boards, the Port of London Authority, the Ministry of Public Buildings and Works and the Metropolitan Water Board. Coordinated by the GLC, they manage to keep the 610 square miles under its jurisdiction reasonably clean and tidy, reasonably healthy and law-abiding (without resort to guns and tear gas) and reasonably well provided with essential services.

The borough councils mend the holes in 7,700 miles of road. They own about 590,000 homes, which they rent out for an average of less than $15 a week each. They maintain about 46,000 acres of parks and sports grounds. About 500 fire engines answer 65,000 calls a year, and 1,000 ambulances each average about seven minutes from call to arrival when picking up the casualties of London life.

The GLC alone spends about $1.4 billion a year. It employs 20,000 teachers in central London to look after 413,000 pupils in 1,098 schools. Every day, it copes with 10,000 tons of garbage and 570 million gallons of sewage. It spends $3.6 million a year on the arts, promotes upward of 1,500 entertainments annually, ranging from automobile racing at Crystal Palace to brass band concerts in Victoria Embankment Gardens, and plants 1.5 million bulbs a year so that Londoners will know when spring has arrived. Without them, it might be hard to tell.

In 1970, the GLC also took on the general responsibility for the London Transport Executive, the world's largest urban passenger transport undertaking. If, as Dr. Johnson observed, there is in London all that life can afford, first you have to get to wherever it's hiding. To do so, Londoners take 2.3 billion passenger trips a year on 6,200 red buses, mostly double-deckers, and 4,000 Underground railway cars, very few of which ever seem to be running in the direction you wish to go.

Life was much simpler for the Romans. All they had to do was march up from the coast of Kent to the Thames marshes in A.D. 43, then follow the river upstream till it narrowed to a bridgeable width. There they proceeded to build Londinium to the greater glory of Rome and the Emperor Claudius.

Some say a Celtic village already stood on the site, near Tower Hill, and that London's first tourists had been fleeced there almost a hundred years earlier, when Caesar's legions came over for a visit two years running. If so, no positive traces remain. There is even a legend about a city called Trenovant built near the Thames in 1100 B.C. by a descendant of Aeneas and later enlarged by King Lud, but again the evidence for so early a settlement is inconclusive.

What *is* certain is that London, by the year 60, was a thriving market town. That was the year when Boadicea, Queen of the Iceni, (more properly known as Boudicca), decided she didn't much care for the place—or the Romans—and burned it down, liquidating the citizenry. (For reasons that remain obscure, this early exercise in social criticism is commemorated by a statue of Boudicca in her chariot at the north end of Westminster Bridge opposite Big Ben and the Houses of Parliament.) The Romans thereupon liquidated Boudicca and the Iceni and rebuilt the city as the commercial center and focus of communications of their British colonies.

In time, London became the largest Roman city in the West, complete with a bridge over the Thames to a suburb in Southwark. And for three centuries more she flourished behind her massive walls, guarded by distant legions holding the ring of empire against the outer darkness. But in 410, the Romans pulled out and the world caved in. London tottered under successive waves of barbarian invaders, surviving the Saxons, falling to the Danes, recovering again under Alfred, then falling once more to the Danes. The times were not propitious for real estate development. London decayed.

But with the arrival of the Normans in 1066, business picked up. The Conqueror, William I, began work on a powerful fortress on Tower Hill to intimidate London but established his court three miles upstream around a bend in the river at the twin city of Westminster, where Edward the Confessor had started to build a great abbey on a gravel bar in the marshes, having moved his government there from Winchester.

It was a fateful step. In the next 600 years, the tensions between the merchants and mob of the walled medieval City and the court and clergy at Westminster were to prepare the ground for the laws and constitutions of half the world. If the lords temporal and spiritual resided at Westminster, the lords commercial and financial lived in the City. The monarch could lop off their heads, but the merchants could lop off his revenues. In the end, the purse proved mightier than the scepter, and to this day, the Queen must still ask the Lord Mayor for permission to enter the City. On ceremonial occasions, she is always met at Temple Bar, by the Law Courts in Fleet Street, to receive from him, symbolically, the City Sword.

With court and commons each striving to curb the other's ambition, the twin cities grew slowly. Outside the City walls, Black Friars, Grey Friars, Templars and Austin Friars founded their monasteries, and the lawyers followed with their inns, the halls, courts and lawns of the Temple, Lincoln's Inn and Gray's Inn stretching north from the river at Blackfriars into Holborn and westward toward Charing, where the mansions and palaces of the great nobles soon lined the river bank, facing the main highway of the Thames. Behind them, the sinks and stews of poverty spread like disease through the smoke and stench of alleys off the Strand, through Holborn and north and east beyond the wall—breeding grounds for a new urban proletariat.

To the south, linked by a narrow-arched bridge top-heavy with tall wooden houses, lay the suburbs of Southwark and Bankside, given over, as time wore on, not just to wharves and warehouses, but to the taverns, theaters and brothels, the bear and pleasure gardens of Shakespeare's and Marlowe's day.

With the 17th century came signs of quickening growth and change. At the Palace of Whitehall, amid the Tudor muddle, a new Banqueting House was started in 1619 by Inigo Jones. Designed in the classic Italian style, it was the first building of its kind to be seen in London, and it still stands, opposite Horse Guards. North of the Strand, the first of the great squares was developed, London's best invention, Covent Garden and Lincoln's Inn Fields. Then another, more northerly still, in Bloomsbury, and yet another, this time in St. James's fields, overlooked from Piccadilly by the grand palaces in the classical manner now being built along the north side. The thread that once linked the City with Westminster along the Strand had thickened into a broad belt.

Then, on the night of September 2nd, 1666, having been wracked by plague for two years, the City burned down. Starting in a baker's shop on Pudding Lane and fanned by an easterly wind, the Great Fire roared through London's timber-framed heart, jumping from street to street for five days, until most of what remained of the medieval city was utterly destroyed.

"All the sky was of a fiery aspect, like the top of a burning oven," wrote John Evelyn in his diary, "and the light seen above forty miles round-about for many nights. God grant mine eyes may never behold the like, who now saw above 10,000 houses all in one flame! The noise and cracking and thunder of the impetuous flames was like a hideous storm. The clouds also of smoke were dismal, and reached, upon computation, near fifty miles in length." In all, some 13,000 houses were burned to the ground and 89 churches, among them the great Gothic cathedral of St. Paul's.

Sir Christopher Wren, mathematician, engineer and architect of genius, devised a scheme for rebuilding the City which would have given London a grandeur and magnificence un-excelled in Europe, but the landlords couldn't wait. Greedy for rents, they threw up new buildings, though this time in brick and to a uniform height, restoring the tortured old pattern of shut-in streets and alleys. Wren's part, in the end, was to rebuild the churches, which he did—51 of them, including the new St. Paul's, his gigantic, magnificent but still humanly scaled triumph.

Meanwhile, new squares had appeared in the West End, in Soho and Gray's Inn fields, and new streets and houses to fill in the spaces. As the first George was crowned, the tempo picked up, starting with Hanover Square and pushing west, and at the Charterhouse and driving east. London was now one city.

In 1760, the last of the City gates came down to prove it. A second bridge spanned the Thames at Westminster and soon a third at Blackfriars. Ribbons of development snaked along the new roads spoking out from the center in all directions to gather in the villages. And still the squares marched on, till a great belt of them stretched from Finsbury to Marylebone and onward toward Bayswater, Brompton and Kensington. The population was now 1¼ millions, having doubled in 100 years.

With the 19th century, the industrial revolution brought thousands of workless in from the country. Dock-building began in the East End. Terraced brown rows of near-instant slums carried London downriver beyond Stepney to the Isle of Dogs. Three new bridges were built in six years, Vauxhall, Waterloo and Southwark. Meanwhile, the great landowners of the West End were completing the spacious, orderly develop-ment of their vast estates: Grosvenor, Cavendish-Harley, Port-man, Portland, Bedford and Southampton. And now it was John Nash, politician, entrepreneur, town planner and archi-tect, who was to put his mark on London as indelibly as Wren had done a century or so before.

With the Prince Regent eager to outshine Napoleon's Paris, Nash drew up a brilliant plan of "metropolitan improvements," and managed to carry most of them out. Marylebone Park, reverting to the Crown in 1811, became Regent's Park, conceived as a rural retreat for the nobility, ringed with elegant terraces and dotted with villas in romantic gardens and groves. Connecting with Robert Adam's Portland Place to the south, a new road, Regent Street, was carved along the borders of Soho and the West End estates, opening up Oxford and Piccadilly Circuses, to link the park with the Regent's palace, Carlton House.

But before the project was anywhere near complete, his patron, now King George IV, decided to convert Buckingham House into Buckingham Palace, and Carlton House, the hinge on which the whole plan turned, was pulled down. On its site, Nash built Carlton House Terrace and Carlton Gardens—the development profits financing his work on the Palace—and St. James's Park was relaid and replanted as the southern counterpart of Regent's Park.

There was still more to come. Having given the West End a backbone, Nash then drew plans for driving Pall Mall eastward from Waterloo Place and cutting a huge square at the head of Whitehall. Christened Trafalgar Square in 1830, it was the last of his great "improvements." Taken together, they are more than an eloquent memorial to the most imaginative of London's planners; they are almost all London has to offer in the grand manner.

After that, with certain honorable exceptions like the Cubitts, Thomas and Lewis, who built Belgravia, Pimlico and much of Bloomsbury, small-minded men increasingly took charge of London's rampaging development. The railway age dawned with a spectacular crop of terminal buildings to speed the flight to the suburbs. The City was largely rebuilt, losing its early Georgian, residential character to a mishmash of styles spiked with the Gothic revival. The West End, also turning commercial as the Georgian leases fell in, was cut about with new streets without quality, like Shaftesbury Avenue and Charing Cross Road. And all the while, the flood tide of semi-detached villas rolled onward and outward, the city's radius doubling between 1850 and 1900.

The Great War of 1914-18 smashed some glass in the City but, more important, broke the spell of complacency. Even the worst of Victorian speculative building had been carried out with confidence—the world's richest city, capital of the greatest empire in history, was not to be judged by any standard but its own. But by 1919, New York was richer, and doubt had set in. Postwar architecture began to look nipped, mean and unsure of itself.

The London County Council, predecessors of the GLC, invented the council house. They pebble-dashed the walls, painted it beige or suicide-green and converted great tracts of Essex into leaden desolation with it. In classier suburbs, developers added a bay window for private buyers and did the same, with occasional excursions into mock-Tudor or mock-Georgian for the carriage trade. Nobody could remember how to build a decent-looking house or relate it to the landscape. Meanwhile, as the sprawl picked up speed—the radius of London doubling again between 1900 and 1930—the East End collapsed into squalor.

Then the Second World War jammed the brake on. The nightly visitations of the Luftwaffe from the late summer of 1940 until well into 1941, and then the final flourish of flying bombs and ballistic missiles in 1944, killed 30,000 people in the city and injured 50,000 more.

V. S. Pritchett remembers in "London Perceived" when "Londoners in the black-out heard the sky grunt, grunt, grunt above them, then howl and rock, or saw it go green instead of black, the whole 700 square miles of it twitching like sick electricity and hammered all over by millions of sharp gold sparks as the barrage beat against it like steel against a steel door. The curling magnesium ribbons that came slowly down were a relief to see, in that unremitting noise. The sky shook London like a rug; the floor boards, the furniture, the pictures, the glasses and plates, the curtains, the favorite vases, ferns, clocks, and photographs, the pens on the desks, the ink in the pots danced in their places throughout the night in evil monotony hard to endure. The sky was extravagant; the earth would occasionally come to life in scattered carroty fires, and on the bad nights, when the docks, the East End, and the City were burned out, the tide being too low to give the firemen water, London turned crimson."

Some 700,000 buildings were hit, of which about a third were completely destroyed.

Battered, shabby and exhausted, London sagged into peace. But remembering the runaway boom of the Twenties, one of the earliest acts of the Labor Government was to corset the city's girth. A metropolitan Green Belt was established around the perimeter, and by and large it still holds.

For a time there was no great pressure on it. The Germans had cleared some big spaces. Most of the City had gone and most of the docks, and with them great swaths of the East End, street after street of slum row houses falling like dominoes away from the points of explosion.

Nothing much else had changed, however. As rebuilding began, it soon became clear that London's architectural Bourbons had forgotten nothing and learned nothing. It was back to the school of domestic anonymous and commercial anonymous, but now in the poverty-stricken idiom of Britain's postwar austerity. Once more an unrepeatable chance to reconstruct the City to a unified grand design was not just missed but barely considered, which may have been just as well since no Wren was about to present himself.

Instead, heavy rectangular office blocks spread over the bomb-fractured clearings around St. Paul's closing off the views. Mainly of colored brick, they were well enough built and respectable but totally lacking in spirit. Designed to offend no one, they pleased no one.

But at least they were low. With the Sixties, confidence returned, though taste remained on holiday. A brash new breed of property speculators began to intrude on the skyline. The style changed from British stolid to international mediocre. Architects discovered glass and poured concrete, if not how to use them, and a rash of new office towers sprouted all over town, some, like Centre Point in St. Giles Circus, to stand empty for years as memorials to greed and the frailty of planners' projections. And as sites provided by courtesy of the Luftwaffe had been long since used up, the developers were now biting hard into the body of Georgian and Victorian London to piece their lots together.

Some of this could be justified—no city can live without change—but most of it could not. Toward the end of the decade, a temporary ban was imposed on new office-building in central London, and it seemed like a victory. But hardly pausing for breath, the property men turned to tower hotels, and the galloping erosion went on.

Except that now resistance is growing. Londoners at last are alarmed—some of them—and long, drawn-out planning procedures allow alarm to be harnessed for action, if the will is there. The mood is changing. Much has been spoiled, more is about to be, but much will remain. The particular quality of London resides in her stupendous totality, in the aggregation of varying neighborhoods, each with its own center, all with their backs to one another. Even now, studded in her unwieldy bulk is the greatest collection of urban masterpieces in Europe, though these are not always seen to their best effect.

There never was any one clearly definable, delicately poised London personality to be upset by boorish intrusions. Set down in the center of Paris, a project like the City's Barbican development would have totally wrecked its character. In London, second-rate architecture is just one more ingredient tossed into the stewpot, gritty but endurable—provided there isn't too much of it.

Chapter Three
. . . as London does

TO DESCRIBE someone as a New Yorker is to pass on a piece of useful information. It places a person psychologically as well as geographically, with its suggestion of restlessness, iconoclasm and self-deprecating egotism. If the melting pot did nothing else, it produced a certain homogeneity of approach to life. But to describe someone as a Londoner suggests nothing, and may even be thought offensive if taken to imply that a person was born there, for in that sense the term has a distinctly low-class connotation. At best, it will evoke one of the many self-serving stereotypes, invented for propaganda purposes or to please tourists, behind which Londoners have sheltered their privacy for years. Believe them, and the city is peopled with indomitable Cockneys, stiff upper-lipped debs and guardees, swinging dollies in kinky boots, tweedy intellectuals, amiable eccentrics and inexpressibly benign custodians of wealth and public virtue.

The truth is, however, that people living in London have little more than that in common; there are few recognizable London types. Compared with the English as a whole, they present no distinguishing attitudes, no collective characteristics as an aid to identification—hardly even in their accents or speech patterns anymore, which are becoming more clearly social than regional. In London, stability is achieved not by a coming together with any sense of common purpose, but by an endless process of subdivision. If the city consists of a thousand villages, then each village comprises a thousand cells. Londoners have learned that the only acceptable way to live together in large numbers is to ignore one another most of the time. They know how to be private even when squashed bosom to buttock in the rush-hour Tube.

This makes their society very difficult for strangers to penetrate, which is the whole idea. Londoners tend to move in small, interconnecting circles of mutual acquaintance based on their homes, work, friends, neighbors, pubs and pastimes. The other seven million or so are just urban wallpaper, as anonymous as the traffic in the streets until a bus breaks down or someone faints and a new group coalesces for a moment around the incident. Whenever two or more Londoners are thrown together, they form a club—a private club to which other members are admitted with increasing reluctance. Even the minor privilege of having witnessed a street accident is not lightly shared in a city where one's individuality is always threatened by the crowd.

This makes generalization very difficult. Perhaps the only safe one is that while Londoners entertain much the same desires, interests and ambitions as anybody else, they are generally less violent about it. Aggressiveness is not particularly admired. Compared with New York, say, self-interest is expressed less nakedly and power abused more subtly. Everything happens within a narrower compass of acceptable behavior. If there's often a touch of desperation about New Yorkers, there's more than a hint of resignation about Londoners.

This, of course, makes an enormous difference in the quality of life. It means that people tend to form orderly lines at bus stops, and bus conductors to derive a quiet satisfaction from leaving as many of them there as possible. It means that whoever usurps your turn to be waited on in a store will probably be very old or French. And above all, it means that Londoners can go pretty well anywhere they choose at any hour of the day or night without fear. They are about as likely to be mugged as they are to find a five-pound note. Neither possibility ever occurs to them.

This is no reflection on London's underworld, of course. She still breeds the most accomplished thieves in the world, but they, too, are expected to play by the rules. No one should get hurt and their victims should be able to afford it. Criminal virtuosity commands the Londoner's grudging admiration; violence or meanness, his ungrudging hostility. It is all right to stick up a bank but not if you use a gun. And when stealing a rich American's wallet, you are supposed to lift it from him in a crowd and not knock him down for it after dark.

This professional restraint helps to make London the safest of all cities to walk around in, day or night. So does good police work and the absence of an army of drug addicts forced to resort to crude or brutal crime in order to support their habits. But the real secret of London's enviable peace and stability is that most Londoners, honest or bent, generally live by a sense of what's fair and right. No legislation can compel consideration for others; where the law leaves off, a kind of natural justice takes over. No one can explain the rules but everyone knows what they are.

A decent concern for life, colored by traditional values and proprieties that begin to seem naive today, works its way through the self-renewing machinery of a society still largely governed by custom and precedent, picks up the conservative bias necessary to sustain the inequities of the class system, and emerges as an elaborate code of behavior which inspires as much bewilderment in foreigners, i.e. non-members, as it does respect. Although its beneficial effects on public order are obvious, how are people expected to know in advance what is "done" and what is "not done"? Why, for instance, is it all right for an advertising executive to send his daughter to riding school and intolerably pretentious for a plumber to do the same? How do they know what is appropriate to their station in life? How, indeed, do they know their station in life?

It begins with childhood. There is something quite frightening about London children. They are an alien race, left out in all weathers, which knows about the adult world and much prefers its own. By themselves, they swoop through the city, intent as wolves, never walking, always on the run, grouping up for collective enterprise in feudally rigid pecking orders of age and strength and daring, disbanding as suddenly for mysterious missions of their own. Stop them in midflight and they will hold a wary distance, skinny, reserved and knowing, and stay no longer than they must. They suffer the grown-up world because they know they are at its mercy; they've been pragmatists from birth. Adults are necessary but not welcome. Though probably fond of their parents, they treat them with condescension or affectionate contempt, expressed as saucily as the balance of power permits. It's not peace, but coexistence.

These are working-class children, of course, for middle-class professional parents can never leave their young alone. Middle-class children meet other nice children for supervised play, go to nice schools under escort, are reasoned with at an early age and generally straggle about trying to learn to like what their parents consider is good for them. The result is often a brat, but of a particular London kind. He is encouraged to think he is special, but not by overindulgence. There is less of that conspicuous consumption of pocket money, chic outfits, power-operated toys and ice-cream sodas which converts New York brats into plump little parodies of Bonwit Teller customers. For one thing, his parents cannot afford it. But more than that, he is special because of the superior sensitivities, the special qualities of character and intellect which his parents believe they have passed on and which clearly befit him for a significant role in society. He is expected to work hard, go to bed early, keep himself fit, learn good manners, practice self-denial, take an intelligent interest in his fellows and in every other way equip himself to take his rightful place among the nation's leaders in government, the professions, business or even, at a pinch, the arts.

Considered like that, in the abstract, this may seem no bad prescription for child-rearing. Encountered in the flesh, however, it explains Britain's reputation for prig-rearing. For what renders these otherwise estimable qualities ultimately bratlike are the side-effects—mock-modesty, unquenchable arrogance and a probably well-founded air of superior knowledge about whatever you happen to be discussing. To be fair, in most other respects they are demonstrably children rather than premature adults. Even the saddest and most precocious remain subject to those immutable laws of childhood which require them, however neat and clean on leaving home, to decompose into scarecrows almost before they are out of sight. For bad vibrations, there is no more upsetting experience for a grown-up in London than to come unaware upon a kindergarten crocodile of junior establishmentarians waiting to cross the street into Kensington Gardens for organized play. Socks wrinkled around their ankles, hats over one ear, expensive little uniforms in wild disarray, they giggle and pinch and pull at each other until the whole column boils with elemental wickedness. Their attendants, generally two of them and either sensible girls who play hockey or muscular matrons in flat hats, make ineffectual calming noises, dash strands of hair from their eyes and gaze despairingly at the traffic, imploring motorists to stop and let their charges across before they get out of hand and sack Kensington High Street.

As anywhere else, it takes a superior person to transcend the circumstances of his upbringing. In London, enough people have managed it to soften the old rigidities of the class system, but even as they zig-zag across its frontiers they know they are doing so. The old order is still honored in the breach; indeed, to speak of "upward mobility" is to acknowledge it. In a middle-class store like Harrods, for instance, shoppers of working-class origin are often identifiable by underlying hints of self-effacement or defiance. When waited on, they are either meek or truculent. Simply being there is a class-conscious act. And in much the same way, when an Old Etonian chooses to drink in the public bar of his local instead of the saloon bar, *his* class credentials are also showing. It takes middle-class assurance to be so careless with status. Not giving a damn, or trying to be *un*class-conscious, are profoundly middle-class traits.

But most Londoners are content to stay where they're put. The working-class child becomes a working-class adult, loyal and easy-going with his mates, on guard and crafty with the bosses. He accepts his social station because he is comfortable in it and because there is nothing wrong with it. He belongs to a class with a strong sense of membership, though weaker than it was; a class that has always prided itself, not without cause, on being the national repository of character, common sense and "real" values. Authority, when it is not actually stepping on his toes, is a bit of a joke. So are middle-class respectability and middle-class materialism. Not much bothered by acquisitive instincts or problems of identity, he is not much driven to compete or even to excel, except in the things that genuinely interest him. He has come to terms with the idea of "us" and "them" and rather enjoys it.

Should he make a killing on the football pools, that splendidly British invention for softening up the masses with the promise of much for little, he will buy his mum and dad a house, replace the black and white telly with a color set, exchange his old Ford (regretfully) for a new one, take his summer vacation in Majorca instead of Ramsgate but otherwise live much as he did before. Similarly with working-class intellectuals, politicians and businessmen. However successful they may become in middle-class terms, they never cease to brag about their backgrounds or display a snobbish passion for jellied eels and dog racing. They wouldn't want anybody to think they were getting above themselves.

In contrast, the middle-class child becomes a middle-class adult who doesn't really *care* what you think—or who manages to give that impression. The British higher-educational system breeds the most pig-headed, argumentative and opinionated people on earth, an offense only partly mitigated by good manners. One of the reasons why senior business management is so often inept is that *real* consultation with subordinates, as distinct from paternalist window-dressing, is widely held to be a sign of weakness or indecision, a dilution of authority. A leader's role is to lead. Though he's learned to express the thought less crudely, having gone to so much trouble to equip himself to run the country, the middle-class professional is damn well not going to have less qualified people meddling in his affairs.

This accounts for the attitude of Tory politicians toward the electorate (and also toward *Labor* politicians). It explains why British doctors treat their patients like idiot children and get quite put out if you insist on learning the details of your own illness, let alone the reason for the therapeutic indignities he means to visit on your person. It sheds light on the callousness of British lawyers who crack little legal jokes with the judges while their clients wriggle in the dock. It is the reason why British shopkeepers appear to hate their customers, why local and national government officials are noticeably less corrupt, why ideals of public service evoke more than cynical guffaws, and why esoteric disciplines are still pursued regardless of their income-earning potential. (London has more high-minded scholars and fanatics per square mile than any less complacent city could tolerate.) Above all, it explains why the British, and London's middle class in particular, have yet to recover from the loss of empire. They were clearly so much better qualified to run the colonies than anybody actually born and raised there.

Everyone agrees the class system is iniquitous but it won't go away. This is probably because everyone finds it so useful. Having "them" in the saddle is a complete alibi for non-achievement ("They never gave me a chance"), for laziness ("Why beat your head against a brick wall?"), and lack of ambition ("Well, somebody's got to collect the garbage").

At the same time it adds virtue to the energetic and successful. Those who manage to beat the system have the additional satisfaction of knowing they've done so against the odds. So why change it? Why rob those coming after them of the same satisfaction? In any case, it would be bad for their characters.

But if there are advantages to being one of "us," they are as nothing to the privilege of being one of "them." At best, it means going to the rat race with a ticket for the grandstand. At worst, it means running as a thoroughbred against a field of pit ponies. Every option is open. No career possibility is closed—except perhaps that of trade union organizer. If you are good at anything, you need never fret about opportunity, for opportunity will seek you out. And if you are good for nothing, you still need not fret, for then it's not *what* you know but *who* you know that counts.

Generations of middle-class administrators have ensured that the output of Britain's top schools and universities will be just about enough to fill the country's top jobs; that the output of its middling schools and redbrick colleges will take care of the middling jobs, and that the rest of the educational system will provide the tradesmen, laborers and unemployment statistics. All are free to cross these lines if they can, just as the rich man is free to lie down in a ditch with a beggar. But whether they do so or not, all are stamped with the marks of their origins and background as plainly as if the information were tattooed on their foreheads. There is nothing they can say, do, wear, eat, drink, buy or even admire that isn't charged with social significance. When bucking the class system, you can sometimes beat them but never join them.

Not everybody plays the game, of course, or finds it useful. Intellectually it's intolerable. But as a focus of discontent, class is such a ritual target, so encrusted with derision, ancient jokes and comic folklore, that not even its victims can take it very seriously. Militants in the class war generally find themselves worn down in a sea of good-natured apathy and, if they don't give up, linger on as licensed eccentrics, sharing the affections of old age pensioners with the Royal Family.

The rest, those who merely dislike the system, tend to opt out into its crevices and create little worlds of their own. Nobody minds. The system can afford a few fleas.

It can even afford to indulge the young in their efforts to set up an alternative society. It took no great acumen to see that their values were commercially vulnerable. Now it's not only who you know but what you wear. In the post-Beatles, post-Carnaby Street era, youth is stuck with a pop hierarchy far more openly and materially status-conscious than the one it was meant to replace. Indeed, the old guard is already combing it through for recruits. Used to being laughed at, it is also used to having the last laugh. Iniquitous perhaps, but what other class structure has endured 900 years without a revolution? (Cromwell doesn't count—his dictatorship was a classic expression of middle-class ideals.) The system survives because it works. Londoners can accept a concentration of power and privilege in the hands of a social élite because they are allowed their self-respect. Unlike 18th-century French and 19th-century Russian autocrats, the British establishment demands only deference, not humility—and then mostly toward the offices of power rather than their occupants. In this way, an attack on class privilege can be represented as an onslaught against the fabric of society, and no one will stand for that.

All of which may sound gloomy and oppressive, but not a bit of it. London is easily the most cheerful of big cities. With everybody's territory staked out, Londoners can concentrate more on making the best of things. Though times are changing, they are still less eaten up with the frustrations that drive people beyond their capacity to cope with life in more competitive societies. Few Londoners spend much time on analysts' couches worrying about their identities. Even if they wanted to, they'd have a hard time finding one, for the shrink industry never really stood a chance in a system which rewards the self-esteem of those who "know their place," which denies no one a chance to count his ignorance as great a virtue as another's knowledge, which values character over cleverness and privacy against profit.

The rich man in his Rolls may feel vastly superior to the common herd, but see who gives way when he meets a poor man driving a London Transport bus. The high court judge may be "m'lud" in the Strand, but in the railway buffet at Waterloo Station he's "luv," "dear" or "ducky" just like the rest of us.

Secure in themselves, Londoners are not afraid to look out for each other. Like any other city, London is as hard as nails, but nobody is deliberately left to make a bed of them. Her citizens are generally patient with the old, considerate of the handicapped, forgiving of the young and devoted to their dogs, who have converted Kensington and other residential districts into one vast canine latrine. On balance, the city seems to have bred the nearest thing yet to a genuinely urban species. It doesn't take much to enlist the sympathy of Londoners, unless, of course, you happen to be a child molester or a colored immigrant.

Race is a blind spot. Only 25 years ago, foreigners were people who came to London to find out how to do things and then went home again. The brown and black ones were either rich or students or both, and there weren't enough of them to upset anybody except a few sexually repressed landladies. At the center of a multiracial empire, Londoners could pride themselves on their tolerance; it was part of the white man's burden.

But in the Fifties, everything changed. The unemployed children of empire decided to try for some of the comforts of home in the Mother Country. Neither rich nor students, they began to arrive in ever-increasing numbers from the West Indies, India and Pakistan and show every sign of settling in, which was another matter entirely. The response, class-inflected as always, ranged upwards from open hostility in working-class districts like Brixton, Notting Hill and Shepherds Bush, where the immigrants clustered most thickly, through the cautious reserve of the lower middle class in areas where they might cluster next, to the sweet reasonableness of the upper middle class, whose progressive wing worried about the ability of the schools and social services to deal with immigrant breeding habits, and whose traditionalists gravely doubted the ability of the police and armed services to avert the inevitable racial bloodbath.

Set against this was the ordinary Londoner's basic fund of decency and the muffling effects of hypocrisy. Though always accounted a national vice, this last has seen the British through many a crisis and helped to keep them civilized. A disinclination to call unpleasant actions by their right names can only come from being aware that such actions *are* unpleasant, and this must necessarily inhibit people with a high opinion of themselves. In the event, nobody's worst fears were realized—at least, not yet. The races, showing no particular desire to integrate, have worked out a *modus vivendi*, a typically British compromise which infuriates purist and bigot alike. All are technically equal before the law, and the only open discrimination now practiced is by the government itself, against West Indians, Indians, Pakistanis and East Africans who want to come to Britain, having been taught they had a right to do so, and who have since been denied entry.

After 15 years of adjustment, Londoners now come in all shades of black, brown and white. As always, they mostly mind their own business and respect one another's territory. Since the Notting Hill riots of 1956, there has been very little violence; a few scuffles here and there on Saturday nights, an occasional skinhead ambush followed by a West Indian reprisal, and that's about all—hardly enough to ruffle the headlines. So far as we know, nobody has yet been killed because of his color. There have been no special problems over employment, housing, education, health or welfare either—none, certainly, that didn't exist already in the crumbling basement of the welfare state. The immigrants took over London's dirtiest jobs and dreariest neighborhoods and their children went to the slummiest schools. And as for their impact on the city's medical and social services, they turned out to be less of a burden than any comparable group of white Londoners.

To put their contribution more positively, if immigrants suddenly took offense at Enoch Powell's disciples and withdrew their labor, the buses and trains would stop running and all the hospitals would close. Streets would go unswept, garbage uncollected and mail undelivered. Indeed, the only essential service completely unaffected would be the Metropolitan Police, who, at last count, had just two West Indian constables. Not that they are discriminating against immigrants, of course. It's just that suitable recruits seem reluctant to come forward because they have somehow gotten it into their heads that the police apprehend black suspects rather more energetically than they do white ones and tend to assume they are guilty until proven innocent.

Outside of this rather specialized relationship, race prejudice in London is expressed by word more than by deed. The sort of language employed quite casually in public places by ordinary respectable folk when referring to immigrants would turn a New York liberal white with fear. London children still play with golliwogs and suburban matrons traditionally favor nigger-brown coats for winter wear. But another generation will probably see an end to it. Most young people either don't see race as an issue anymore or are thoroughly bored with it. And so far as London-born black teenagers are concerned, a bigot trying to insult them on racial grounds would probably have to explain that that was what he had in mind in order to avoid having the attempt written off as conventional adult bitchiness. The young Jamaican conductor who tried to help a middle-aged white woman board his 73 bus in Park Lane and who kept grabbing for her arm as she eluded him, apparently fearing rape, laughed as hard as anyone when she finally fell off in the road on her well-upholstered behind.

Often it's xenophobia more than race. The Londoner who reacts irrationally to dark skins is just as likely to be offended by Spanish accents, Italian gestures or Irish flamboyance. He is the sort who stands heroically at attention in movie theaters when they play a few perfunctory bars of the national anthem after the last performance, trembling with fury as everyone else dives for the exits, and organizes petitions in his lighter moments to bring back flogging and capital punishment. Fortunately, there aren't enough of him to count, but he does represent in a highly exaggerated, not to say neurotic, way the muted nationalism which colors the outlook of most Londoners brought up before the last world war in Britain's imperial sunset.

Patriotism is too positive a term to describe it, and too embarrassing for anybody but a fox-hunting Tory M.P. from a Gloucestershire constituency to mention in public. The word induces uncontrollable giggles in the young, and the middle-aged have become as furtive about it as they once were about sex. But the pride of belonging is still there, just below the surface, a pride of membership much like that which informs the working class, ex-public (private) schoolboys, commuters on the 8:15 from Woking and football club supporters. To be British is to be quietly and sensibly superior. Generations of them have minded the world's business as if it were their own. Millions have gone off to the wars and died in mild astonishment that foreigners had actually learned how to make bullets.

Visitors to London content to flit like mayflies between the sights will probably never know this. Most Londoners are nice to foreigners on vacation because they are fair-minded enough to realize they are not being foreign on purpose. Difficulties with the money, or the language or in getting around town will elicit a tolerant smile, a kind word and, at worst, an amused shake of the head. But if the visitor digs in deeper, as he should, to get to know the natives, he may, unless he is careful, find himself picking his way through a conversational minefield—particularly if he comes from a country as touchy and as idiotically self-centered as theirs.

To avoid refueling traditional rumors of anti-Americanism, for instance, all but the most emancipated should avoid gossiping in saloon bars about the two world wars, postwar American foreign policy and the sanctity of the dollar. Nothing new will emerge, as Mr. Bernard J. Gomberg, of New York City, discovered when his first visit to London coincided with the international dollar crisis. In an indignant letter to *The Evening Standard*, one of London's two afternoon papers, he wrote:

"Thirty years ago, we Americans gave our money and our blood to save your country, and now you have missed the greatest chance to prove to America and the entire world that Britain is the true partner of America in the free world. The American dollar should have been backed by the Bank of England to the last cent.

"Where are you now when all the world looks to you as you discount American dollars? Shame on you. We gave our lives to save you. You will not give a few new pence to prove to the world that we are not finished."

It may be that *The Standard*, whose love of foreigners is equalled only by that of the *Daily News* in New York, published this familiar American complaint of British ingratitude in order to provoke the familiar British complaint of American ingratitude. If so, its confidence was not misplaced in A. W. Field, of Beckenham, Kent, who rose in reply like St. George:

"Mr. Gomberg," he wrote, "while England hung on alone against Germany, she did not save America, she saved the world. Only the Japanese and Pearl Harbor could lure you from your home.

"A population of 45 million was insufficient to finish the job, and an island roughly twice the size of New York state could not carry out the task alone, but unlike the United States, who waxed rich in the task, we were battered and bankrupted by the effort.

"As to your generosity, we are still paying the interest on those magnanimous gifts of money for the First and Second World Wars. We have not yet started on the capital.

"As to your blood, left to you—as the rate of progress in Vietnam has shown—we would still be at war with the Kaiser. Creep back to your desert, push your head firmly in the sand and never again try to teach granny how to suck eggs."

One may safely assume that Mr. Field, like Mr. Gomberg, is around 50—and that in his local pub that night, every customer over the age of 35 offered to buy him a drink. The younger ones could hardly have known what the exchange was all about. They will either have scored one for Britain in some dimly understood competition for international status, like ocean yacht racing, or written it off as another boring display of middle-aged incomprehension of the real issues of the day.

London's young are, on the whole, much freer than their parents, less burdened with the past, less socially inhibited. British reserve, so often compounded of stuffiness and parochialism, lingers on in first-class railway carriages, but is rapidly being replaced by a tacit understanding that privacy consists in being left alone because you want to be, rather than because you haven't been introduced. In dress, manners and deportment, London is now less formal than New York by far, though the old proprieties are still observed at royal garden parties, Jewish weddings and in places like the Connaught Hotel, which won't admit women in slacks to its dining rooms, and the Ritz, which refuses tea in the palm court to men without ties. Almost everywhere else, almost anything goes, including Covent Garden opera house, where people have actually been seen wearing evening dress.

But social inhibitions can cut both ways. Some are worth

keeping. The only uneasy moment anyone is likely to have on a London street, apart from looking the wrong way when stepping off the curb, is on meeting a gang of adolescents, high on beer or excitement and egging each other on to accost girls, kick over garbage cans and similar feats of daring. Though these encounters are rare on tourist territory, and hardly ever amount to more than a minor nuisance anyway, hooliganism *is* getting to be a problem.

Every Saturday afternoon during the soccer season London's stadiums are guarded as if somebody meant to steal them. Policemen in cars, vans and buses, on foot, horses and motorcycles are deployed outside in massive numbers to keep the fans in check, both coming and going. Though most of them are orderly enough, there is something about soccer that agitates its more impressionable supporters to the borders of hysteria. It has become an emotionally charged war game, with two embattled teams of gladiators cheered on by perhaps 30,000 rabid partisans only too willing to continue hostilities afterwards in the streets. Hardly a week goes by during the season without some sort of incident, if not of near-riot then of property damage by roving bands of young toughs working their fever out on the neighborhood.

Why soccer, a relatively mild game in terms of physical contact between players, should arouse such warlike passions when rugby football, a harder, rougher game, will produce little more than an epidemic of sore throats is something of a mystery. Class again, probably. Big-league soccer is played by working-class professionals; big-time rugby by middle-class amateurs, at least in the south of England. One taps the emotive power of local patriotism working on loyalist groups so identified with their champions that their very self-esteem depends on the outcome of the match; the other engages the high spirits of fans with nothing personal at stake, except perhaps in international matches. The game's the thing, or so they say. For them, to be lost in the crowd is a pleasing diversion and not a way of life.

London's summer sports fit her decorous image better. Fanaticism is hard to sustain when a game lasts three days, with breaks for lunch and tea. Cricket at Lord's· or the Oval probably comes closer than anything else to those romantic notions of London cherished by people who have never been there or who went into exile long ago. On a dreamy August

day, with a warm sun in a speckled sky and a fitful breeze
from the southwest, there is no gentler way to reconciliation
with life than to push through the turnstiles at Lord's, the
prettier of the two grounds, rent a green and red plastic
cushion and settle in on the bleachers at the Nursery end.

For the foreigner, most of what passes between the players
in the middle will seem as enigmatic as Chinese opera, but it
doesn't matter. When everything works—the sunlight, cool
air, the summer sound of trees, old men dozing, executives
lazing, schoolboys out with their fathers, distant murmurs
from the Tavern, patters of applause, white figures sedate
upon a field of gaudy green—when everything hangs together,
Lord's can yield up a bit of the English essence. It's full of
comfortable certainties. This is how things were and are and
should be. This is the rock amid shifting sands.

Wimbledon is another matter, a greener Forest Hills with
strawberries and cream on the lawn. The crowds are thicker
here, but still polite and mostly female, for tennis is taught
to girls in school as cricket is taught to boys. Adjustments
come later, as one might expect with an educational system
still largely segregated by sex.

This applies to other sports, too. Londoners are left with a
lot to learn about each other in adult life, and often apply
themselves to the task in public places with a vigor which
shocks strait-laced visitors, like the French. The parks in summer look like battlefields, strewn with the fallen, all cut down
in pairs.

London is no Copenhagen, of course, but neither is she the
repressed spinster of Franco-American myth. Sex is now quite
widely recognized as one of the facts of life. Girls are perhaps
inclined to tease with some of the things they wear, or almost
wear, and admiring strangers have been known to complain
later that appearances promised more than was actually delivered. But the girls could no doubt say the same of many
admiring strangers, and certainly the local lads don't seem to
mind. Perverse it may be to advertise the goods then feign
indifference to the customers, but the haughty progress of a
booted, micropanted, bra-less dolly down King's Road on a
Saturday afternoon, or past a construction site any day of the
week, invariably provokes a running fire of comment and by-
play immensely satisfying to all concerned.

London's irrepressible bawdiness has at last fatally breached

the Victorian tradition of public prudery and private pruri-
ence, although enough remains to inspire occasional, absurd
prosecutions for obscenity and to allow those who genuinely
don't want to be bothered by unsolicited gropings and pinch-
ings to move about more freely than they ever could in Rome
or Tel Aviv. Sex is out in the open again, and not just in porn
shops, strip clubs and skin flicks, 42nd-Street-style, but everywhere, explicitly. Advertisers sell with it, popular newspapers
and magazines build circulation on it and even dear old
Aunty BBC, a public corporation very conscious of its re-
sponsibilities toward a family audience, allows its television
producers a license in matters of language, nudity, situation
and subject matter that would result in one long bleep on
CBS or NBC.

And yet it's all very cozy and easy to live with. Sophistication is rarely permitted to become a drag or to degenerate
into mere chic. Smart London women, for instance, could
never be confused with smart New York women; most of
them are too healthy and too careless ever to look as if they
were synthesized between the pages of *Vogue*. In much the
same spirit, their husbands still make jokes about "my other
suit," even when they own a third or fourth. Conspicuous
consumption is considered bad form, not because Londoners
enjoy mortifying the flesh—quite the opposite—but because
the effort of providing for greater consumption might get in
the way of the gardening. The thought is not often expressed
in such terms, of course. Modest expectations, a willingness
to settle for less than what's there, are widely regarded as
meritorious—and nowhere more fervently than in the board-
rooms of industry, which take merciless advantage of it. But
of all the reasons advanced to explain why Londoners rarely
go to extremes, none is more convincing than that they are
mostly too lazy.

So there they stand—if all these generalizations are to be
believed—clannish, sly, snobbish, class-ridden, cynical, complacent, racist, hypocritical, xenophobic, sloppy, vandalistic,
effete, immoral and dowdy layabouts. Such are the difficulties,
already noted, of finding something broadly true to say about
seven and a quarter million dedicated individualists.

To correct so many generalizations naturally calls for another one. Londoners are also the gentlest, kindest, cheeriest

breed of city-dwellers alive. And long may they keep their patience with the eight million visitors who get under their feet every year and who may, if they keep their eyes and ears open, learn something to their advantage.

Chapter Four

. . . wising up

*A*SK A taxi-driver to take you downtown and you are liable to wind up at a boutique of that name on Kensington High Street. The expression isn't used in London. There is no downtown. Or if you prefer, *everything* is downtown north of the River Thames between Putney and the City. London is very spread out.

And there's another confusing thing. London is *a* city, but *the* City is something else. *The* City of London is the financial district, the tangled square mile by Tower Hill where God met Mammon and lost, leaving 40-odd churches that close on Sundays. And as if that weren't confusing enough, most of the rest of tourist London is in the City of Westminster, which is not really a city at all but a borough, like the Royal Borough of Kensington and Chelsea, which is not really as royal as Westminster, which contains the Palace of Westminster, which is not really a palace at all, and Buckingham and St. James's Palaces, which are.

Apart from that and a few other local idiosyncrasies like coy little street nameplates and the fact that four consecutive right turns will hardly ever bring you back to where you started, London is no more of a problem than any other city laid out without regard for logic, the laws of navigation or the sanity of tourists. The important thing is to have a destination in mind. Traveling to it by public transport will be the least of your problems, provided you don't actually want to get there. If you do, take a taxi.

There are four main ways of getting around town: on foot, which is quite the best method for sightseeing; on the top deck of a bus, which is next best; by the Underground railway (Tube) which is easily the fastest and most boring, and by taxi. Cars and bicycles are readily available for hire but cannot be recommended for visitors of nervous disposition used to driving on the right (i.e. *wrong*) side of the road. In prime tourist territory, travel by any method between the rush hours of 8 a.m. and 9:30 a.m. and 4 p.m. and 6 p.m. will be purgatory, especially when it's raining. The big exception to this is Oxford Street, which is purgatory all the time, regardless of the weather.

On foot, you will need Geographers' 6-inch scale map of Central London (or Geographers' New A to Z Atlas of London if you are foraging farther afield) and a paperback copy of David Piper's "The Companion Guide to London." When in doubt, don't hesitate to stop a passing Londoner and ask. Most of them are glad to help. And even those who aren't can rarely resist a chance to display their superior knowledge. The only trouble is that at the height of the season you are likely to stop a procession of non-English-speaking Continentals even more hopelessly lost than you are. And take a raincoat. Except in really settled spells, the weather can run through its seasonal repertoire in a single afternoon.

Traveling by bus, the first step is to establish which route or routes you want. There are dozens of them. London Transport publishes a computer circuit diagram which it tries to pass off as a free bus map, but makes up for this with a Travel Enquiries service (222-1234) which will be delighted to give you a busy signal most of the time. Anyway, it's more fun to unravel these mysteries at first hand.

Most bus stops have panels on both sides giving the routes of the buses that stop there. If your destination isn't listed, you can either consult a fellow traveler waiting in line, which could land you in Tooting, or apply to the conductor of the first bus that comes along. Having found a stop with the right route number, you still have two points to watch: first, that your bus is going *toward* and not away from your destination (it's easy to make this mistake; buses with the same number travel in both directions and you are, after all, waiting on the wrong side of the street), and second, that if you are standing at a red "Request" stop, you signal the driver in good time by extending your left arm. Otherwise your bus will very likely go sailing on by and you'll have another 20 minutes to wait for the next one.

After that, it's easy. You can smoke upstairs if you want to, and if you ask him nicely, the conductor will tell you when to get off. (He will tell you to get off at the next stop if you *have* made a mistake, but without charging you for it.) Fares vary according to distance, and you must keep your ticket handy in case an inspector gets on and wants to see it. Londoners are about equally divided between those who swear by the buses and those who swear *at* them—routes 9, 11, 73 and 74 are universally execrated—but everybody agrees it just won't be the same in 1980 when the conductors are gone and the new one-man buses take over.

In comparison, going by Tube is child's play. Even foreigners can read the Underground map. Most places north of the river are served by its eight lines, the trains are quick, clean and comfortable, and there is absolutely no reason why tourists should ever want to use them unless they are late for appointments on the other side of town. Once is all right, just to see how much better the Tube is than American subway systems, but after that it is simply perverse to have traveled so far just to burrow about below ground. (Do not be misled, by the way, by signs reading "Subway." This will only take you under the street and up on the other side.)

Fares are again based on distance traveled, with a minimum of 5p, the tickets being dispensed from a booth or by machine. They are either green, which means you go through a gate manned by a ticket collector, or yellow, which means you have to feed them into automatic turnstiles, which return them at the start and keep them at the finish of each journey. It is technically illegal to board a train without a ticket—indeed, impossible with the automated system—but if you don't know the fare and there's a long line at the booth, buy a 5p machine ticket and pay the difference, if any, at the other end. The ticket will show where you got on, so the amount won't be open to negotiation.

Taxis are best. And after midnight, there's nothing else anyway. Their boxy shape is not only a London trademark but a mark of civilization. They are nimble in traffic; absurdly cheap by New York standards, starting at 15p on the clock; you can get in and out without risking a disk or a coronary, and the drivers don't feel obliged to entertain you with light conversation about their hernias. The drawbacks are those of taxi services everywhere. You can't get one immediately before or after lunch or at theater time and they apparently melt in the rain. In London, they also disappear between 5 p.m. and 6 p.m. to change drivers. Sooner than quarrel over the spoils of this peak-hour business, the day men and the night men both renounce it. This is a classic example of the British genius for compromise. Both parties agree to victimize a third party, in this case, the traveling public.

Otherwise, most London taxi-drivers are a pleasure to do business with. They know the city backwards—before they can get a license they have to pass a searching police examination known as "the knowledge" on routes, street names and landmarks—and there are few better sources of information on where the action is. Tips normally range from 15 per cent to 20 per cent of whatever's on "the clock," with a minimum of 5p, plus whatever you think their advice is worth. They are very broad-minded, especially the young ones.

If shopping is the kind of action you've got in mind, it's Oxford Street for run-of-the-mill department stores, plus the Marks & Spencer flagship branch at the Marble Arch end; Regent Street for a better-class big-store trade, including the fabulous Liberty's; Bond Street for expensive specialty stores; Piccadilly for Fortnum & Mason or Jackson's, the Queen's grocers, and Jermyn Street for shirts and Paxton and Whitfield's cheese shop.

Off dead center, to the west, is the Knightsbridge-Sloane Street-Brompton Road complex, where trendies mingle with the upper crust in Harrods and Beauchamp Place boutiques. And from the southern end of Sloane Street, King's Road beckons the well-heeled traveler into a cloud-cuckoo land of high-priced tat and gear that peters out in Parsons Green. The tat trade has also taken root on Kensington Church Street and Kensington High Street, thanks to Biba the trail-blazer, and Mr. Freedom's liberated chicks now leaven the lumpish dowagers of Barker's and Derry & Toms, London's squarest department stores. It was characteristic of Barker's general outlook on life when, during a recent power strike, they shut down half their escalators in a public-spirited attempt to conserve electricity. Which half? The up side, naturally.

These, then, are the principal, concentrated shopping neighborhoods, but there are tens of thousands of stores all over town, and half the fun of plodding around on foot is the pleasure of discovery. There are also the streets that specialize: Charing Cross Road for books; Carnaby Street for trash; Camden Passage, Westbourne Grove and Portobello Road for antiques shading into bric-a-brac, junk and trivia.

Stores are usually open six days a week from 9 a.m. or 10 a.m. to 5 p.m. or 6 p.m., with late night shopping on Wednesdays or Thursdays. Some still close at 1 p.m. on Saturdays—including John Lewis on Oxford Street and Peter Jones on Sloane Square, London's nearest equivalents to Bloomingdale's—and early-closing days, either Wednesday or Thursday at 1 pm, are still observed in fringe shopping districts, including the King's Road (Thursday). Tourists can avoid paying Purchase Tax on everything they buy if they arrange for the store to deliver the goods to the airport or mail them to their home addresses. This can save up to 20 per cent on many gift items.

Portobello Road does most of its business on Fridays and Saturdays, when it turns into London's best-known open-air flea market and hippie hangout. Although prices are generally lower than they would be in, say, New York, assuming the same kind of stuff could be found there, there are few real bargains. On the other hand, traders know it pays to let their customers think they are stealing from them and set their prices higher to allow for a little haggling. Nobody should be in too much of a hurry to settle, therefore. This also applies in Camden Passage and the antique supermarket warrens on Barrett Street, Kensington High Street and King's Road.

A lot of the stuff they sell in these places comes from the "professional" markets—the Caledonian in Bermondsey Street, which opens at dawn every Friday and is usually shopped out by 10 a.m., and, for really low-end merchandise, the Totters' Market, open at 7 a.m. on Sundays off Middlesex Street. Here, the last of London's itinerant junkmen try to unload whatever the early-bird dealers won't take onto the enormous crowds that later on pack into Petticoat Lane, most famous of all London street markets. It's no use looking for Petticoat Lane on the map, by the way, because it isn't there. This impossibly Cockney-Jewish-Oriental bazaar is centered on Middlesex Street but slops over in all directions. And while in the neighborhood, on a Sunday morning, you might also have a look at Club Row, which doesn't exist either. This is Sclater Street, an open-air market for pets—puppies, kittens, birds, reptiles and occasionally more exotic beasts—but not for the chicken-hearted. Relax your guard for one moment and you could find yourself declaring a cross-bred Labrador and a clutch of goldfish to U.S. Customs.

There are two things worth remembering on these and similar expeditions. One is that London's almost totally undeserved reputation for bad food has been sustained in recent years by Wimpy bars, Texas/Kentucky/Tennessee Pancake Heavens, The Golden Egg, Lyons, Jolyon (Son of Lyons), London or Angus Steak Houses and sundry other chain or franchise operations, often libelously pretending to American origins. For light refreshments and resting the feet, even the Italian cafes are better. There are hundreds of these everywhere, all recognizable by their steam Wurlitzer coffee machines, and here at least you will get bad food with personal service. During licensing hours, the pubs, as always, are best, but failing that, a bit of adroit planning can insure that coffee and tea breaks are taken at strategic locations—Fortnum & Mason's Fountain, Derry & Toms Roof Garden, Bendicks on Wigmore Street, Maison Bertaux on Greek Street, Gloriette opposite Harrod's, Claridge's, Brown's, the Ritz or, indeed, any of the better-class hotels.

The second thing is that, unlike prudish American cities, London makes adequate provision for disposing of refreshments once you've finished with them. Not comfort stations nor powder rooms nor men's rooms, they are Public Lavatories or Public Conveniences, clearly marked MEN and WOMEN or, in superior districts, GENTLEMEN and LADIES. Though they are drafty in winter, it is no disgrace to be seen going into one. Even the best people use them. They are generally clean, safe and graffito-free (more or less), and some of the Victorian ones in Holborn and the City are minor works of art, what with their marble, mahogany and polished brass piping. WOMEN (or LADIES) have to pay, hence the genteel euphemism, "to spend a penny." But as with everything else recently, the price has gone up.

Next to taxi-drivers, who tend to specialize in basics, the best sources of information about what's on are *Time Out*, an uninhibited weekly magazine available at most newsstands; 246-8041, which provides a taped daily summary of London events; and the newspapers, especially the tabloid *Evening Standard*. Nine morning and two afternoon papers are published on Fleet Street, ranging politically from the mandarin *Daily Telegraph* to the Moscow-aligned Communist *Morning Star*. Unlike their American contemporaries, for whom, with honorable exceptions, news is a commodity for holding the ads and gossip columns apart, they are all produced to a high technical standard, and some, *The Guardian, The Times* and the pink (in color, not politics) *Financial Times* are extremely readable. None of them publishes on Sunday, when their places are taken by a comparable group of weekly papers strung out across an equally broad spectrum of political outlook and literary merit, headed by *The Sunday Times* and *The Observer*.

American visitors often find this excellent variety bewildering. Sitting around in the lobby of the Hilton waiting for something to happen, nice middle-aged, middle-class, middle-Westerners uncomprehendingly turn the pages as if they were printed in Esperanto. Only *The Herald Tribune*, printed in Paris and flown over every morning, seems to strike a spark. Its combined Saturday/Sunday editions carry the current *New York Times* weekend crossword puzzle. Perhaps more to the point, it also prints the previous day's closing prices on Wall Street.

But television is the great leveler. Now that so much of the BBC's output is being sold to the American networks, and so much of theirs is coming back in return, London television is a sure cure for homesickness, but still different enough to be interesting. There are three channels, BBC 1 and 2 and a commercial channel occupied on weekdays by Thames Television and by London Weekend from Friday night to Sunday night. Except for odd programs, the BBC finds it absurdly easy to run rings around them both, although there is a certain melancholy pleasure in watching commercials for the same old products rehearse the same old lies and insincerities in a different accent.

Transmissions on BBC 1 and Thames or Weekend begin around 2 p.m., with children's, school or sports programs filling in the afternoon until the main schedule begins around 6 p.m. BBC 2 swings in with its heavier-weight contribution at 7:30 and all three will have closed down shortly before or after midnight. At the weekends, programs start earlier—actually in the morning on Sundays—and maybe they'll throw in a couple of movies in the afternoon. Documentaries, current affairs, magazine programs and drama are the things to watch —and dramatized serials especially. The BBC has made these its own distinctive and highly compelling art form, as Mr. Joseph Sachs of Philadelphia, Pennsylvania, can testify. Unwary enough to catch the first two weekly episodes of Aldous Huxley's "Eyeless in Gaza" in the course of an eight-day visit, he found himself so completely hooked that he had to stick around for four weeks to see the thing through.

Radio is something else. The BBC, whose monopoly will finally be broken with the arrival of local commercial stations in 1973, broadcasts on one AM, one FM and three AM/FM channels. Radio 1, the pop station, features a string of frantically cheerful DJ's nearing middle age who are apparently out to blow the mind of every shop assistant in Streatham. Their task is not made any easier by the Musicians' Union, which limits them to so much record, or "needle," time per day. The gaps are plugged, in every sense, by gushing fan interviews with pop personalities and by live groups whose ambition often outruns their musicianship.

Radio 2 is for *hausfraus* with their vacuum cleaners on, and Radio 3 for civilization—a steady diet of music, spiced with poetry and drama in the evenings, often splendidly experimental, and lectures on Sumerian pottery markings. Radio 4 is talk, talk, talk—for schools, for mothers with young children, for the aged or bedridden who like to be read to, and for anyone else who would otherwise rarely hear a human voice. The FM station, Radio London, combines the worst features of the other four. It does, however, keep everybody up-to-date with the day's events, traffic hold-ups, the weather and how the commuter trains are running.

Armed with all this useful information, the phone number of the British Tourist Authority (629-9191), the knowledge that temperatures average 35 degrees F in winter and 70 degrees in summer, that Marks & Spencer is best for sturdy, inexpensive umbrellas, that service is often included in restaurant bills, so be careful not to tip twice (15 per cent is plenty), that deck chairs in the parks cost 5p a session, that it's okay for a woman to go into a pub alone, and that "pardon" doesn't always mean "excuse me" but more often "What did you say?", the visitor is now ready to meet the most placid yet least predictable of cities, if not exactly on equal terms, then at least with an even chance of finding out why 60,000 other Americans gave up on their home towns to settle there.

Chapter Five

. . . out of sight

*T*HE ONE panoramic view of London that isn't spoiled by the Hilton Hotel is from the Rooftop Bar of the Hilton Hotel. That and fresh orange juice and American coffee are all that can be offered in mitigation of an otherwise indecent assault on the London skyline. And if it seems unfair to keep harping on one such crime among so many, the Hilton was the first of the tower hotels and therefore enjoys the same sort of distinction as Cain does among fratricides.

Tall buildings have no context in London. For centuries, the city fathers preserved her human scale by holding the roofline down. When seeking to impress, they dealt in mass and proportion and richness of ornament, not height. The sky, arching uninterrupted from horizon to horizon, belonged to God, and only the great church-builders like Wren and Hawksmoor were allowed to reach for it, in a spirit of homage and aspiration.

But the Swinging Sixties changed all that. When Harold Macmillan told the British they'd never had it so good, he was thinking of London's landlords. In the new Tory age of enlightenment, gimcrack towers sprouted all over the city, in homage and aspiration to fatter rents. Dwarfing everything around them, these king-sized money boxes exposed themselves in public with the furtive bravado of men in shabby raincoats on the subway. But only the very best erections can justify that kind of self-display, and most of these were flaccid.

For one thing, they bore about as much relationship to London as giant plastic gnomes would bear to the gardens of Versailles. There being no native tradition of high-rise building to sustain them, British designers had to draw heavily on

47

foreign experience, often adapting what they borrowed to awkward sites, different construction methods, unsuitable materials and penny-pinching clients. The result was a bastard crop of architectural mutants, unassimilably alien and impossible to hide. Standing alone, like the Hilton, they jut from the ground like dead teeth. In clumps, as with the City's Barbican project, they desolate the spirit, generating none of the excitement that even third-rate buildings seem to catch from one another in Manhattan. Instead of raising the pulse, the Barbican flattens the mind with a brutal waste of poured concrete.

In fact, there is probably only one high-rise building in all of London which has given more than it has taken away, and that's the Post Office Tower, an honest joke, a technological folly to spice the view, a success because it doesn't pretend to be something it's not, and 620 feet high because it *has* to be, in order to serve its purpose as a microwave relay station.

Shiny green and gray by day and spangled with colored lights at night, it rears up from a muddle of job-lot construction just west of Tottenham Court Road like a colossal space ship stalled on its launch pad. The effect is so comically at odds with any reasonable expectations a visitor might bring to an ancient city that it raises a smile; it entertains where buildings like Portland House at Victoria or Centre Point at St. Giles Circus or Vickers Millbank Tower merely depress or irritate.

On a fine day, the Post Office Tower also provides the best vantage point for tourists too lazy to use their feet. Above the observation galleries, there's a cocktail bar and a revolving restaurant which serves a poor but expensive lunch while patrons watch the sights drift by three times an hour, as if sitting on the axis of the world.

But London yields few secrets from above. An ascent of the Eiffel Tower will certainly help unlock the grand design of Paris, but there are no such revelations to be had 600 feet over London—just a bewildering impression of size and random geometry. She takes shape and makes sense only on the ground, in sequences of closed views, some long, some short, —and all different. If Paris is a great urban canvas, London is a string of miniatures, a cartoon strip, changing in character and mood from frame to frame—now grand, now domestic; now beautiful, now squalid.

She's a tough proposition for any visitor who isn't content to be shipped around like a parcel to gawk on cue at the standard sights. People who want to approach London, not as a museum with shopping facilities, but on a human, more intimate level will find her baffling and her quality elusive if they simply turn themselves loose on the town. They'll need purpose and direction, some thread of interest to follow if, in the end, they're not to be pursued home by the nagging suspicion that for every discovery they made there were a dozen more they missed—perhaps better ones.

Nothing can safely be taken for granted, not even the ride into town on arrival. The road from Heathrow, like almost every other highway connecting a big city with its airport, runs through suburbs resembling Queens. The seasoned traveler is resigned to this and pays no attention. The first-time visitor tries not to look, delaying that long-awaited first impression for something worthy of it—which, on the airport bus, won't happen much before Chelsea. And so both of them will probably miss the first solid clue to the nature of London. About 50 yards short of the Chiswick traffic circle, on the right-hand side of the road, the poky little late 17th-century house where William Hogarth lived is jammed up against the backside of a huge 20th-century shoe-polish factory.

From then on in, it's incongruity all the way. Hogarth's House is a few yards from the gates of Chiswick House, Lord Burlington's sumptuous 18th-century palace in the Palladian manner which has some of the most spendidly decorated rooms in Europe. But there's nothing to see from the road. There's nothing to see at the traffic circle either, except drivers playing Russian roulette, and yet leading off it is a quiet village lane so coyly picturesque that Walt Disney might have built it. This is Church Street. It runs down to the bank of the Thames, past the church of St. Nicholas, where Hogarth is buried (and Burlington, too) and turns left at the water's edge to become Chiswick Mall, a peaceful stretch of pretty Georgian houses overlooking the river as it runs on down towards Hammersmith. And about 100 yards to the north, busloads of tourists are grinding along on a parallel course wondering where the sights begin.

London is like that. You never quite lose the feeling that you're just a street away from something marvelous, and most of the time, you are. But short of devoting a lifetime to

these mysteries, which isn't a bad idea either, the visitor determined to carry off a true and orderly impression of her
must somehow subdue all this troublesome variety, and
establish a sense of perspective.

Perhaps the best way to start is to plot a ruthless five-mile
radius from Trafalgar Square and forget the rest, at least to
begin with. A 50p London Transport sight-seeing bus tour will
then, in a mere two hours, set out most of the standard
tourist attractions and establish the rough geographical relationship between them. The irreducible minimum consists of
Buckingham Palace, Westminster Abbey, the Houses of Parliament, the National Gallery, the British Museum, St. Paul's and
the Tower. Duty done, visitors are then free to concentrate on
those that appealed to them most, bearing in mind that any
one of these heavyweights can take up to a half-day in itself.

If this is too much, if they find the Abbey, for instance,
gorged with tourists, as it usually it—more than five million
people shuffled doggedly through in 1971—they should be content to admire it from the outside, as most Londoners do,
and take a pleasantly unflurried hour to look at some of the
other treasures tucked away in that quarter of Westminster.
Similarly with the Tower. About two and a half million people trudge up and down the staircase of the Bloody Tower
every year, and no doubt they consider it worth the trouble.
But if more discriminating travelers have no particular desire
to get their heels tramped on, they can instead enjoy a dozen
uncrowded pleasures within half a mile and in about the same
space of time.

If St. Paul's is crowded, try St. Stephen Walbrook or St.
Margaret Lothbury or St. Mary Abchurch. They'll probably be
empty, and everyone should see them anyway. St. Paul's is a
masterpiece, but so are these. And if it seems a pity not to
watch the Changing of the Guard at Buckingham Palace after
coming so far, it's no less a pity to lose most of a morning
jockeying for position with upward of 12,000 other people—
especially when the City of Westminster has estimated that
only about 3,500 can see in reasonable comfort. A better bet by
far, when the Queen is out of town, is to catch the Changing
of the Guard at *St. James's Palace*—in Friary Court at 10:30
a.m.

So if the British Museum or the Victoria and Albert is
overrun, try Sir John Soane's Museum in Lincoln's Inn Fields

or the London Museum in Kensington Palace. They're not the
same but they're as good in their way. And when the Cheshire
Cheese is full for lunch, try the George and Vulture or Simpson's Tavern (the one in the City, not in the Strand). And if
you can't face the scrum in Fortnum & Mason's, go buy your
plovers' eggs at Harrods, whose *art nouveau* shrine to high-
class butchery and fishmongering is as fine an interior as
London can offer.

In short, there is simply no need to waste time in confronta-
tions with the herd; the city can cope comfortably with everyone provided they spread themselves out. It's one of the
few places where taking the line of least resistance doesn't
necessarily mean settling for second best.

Having cased the joint by bus, then, the intelligent sightseer's next step is to settle on a short list of places for
closer inspection, backed up with plenty of alternative targets
in the vicinity, a good street map and an umbrella. As one
man's feat is another man's boredom, much will depend on
personal tastes and interests. But there are some views, some
buildings and some combinations of the two that are of the
very essence of London, often much closer to it, indeed, than
the tourist set-pieces, and these should not be missed by anybody who really wants to remember where he's been.

Around the Tower

TO START AT THE TOWER, if whiny kids are pulling at weary
mums while ice cream wrappers fall like autumn leaves,
resolve to come back in winter or at 10 o'clock sharp next
morning and cross the street to Trinity Square. On the north
side, ponderously overborne by the Port of London Authority
Building, is S. Wyatt's delectable Trinity House, whose unobtrusive good manners repay attention, and, to the east, a
massive hunk of Roman wall, about 50 feet long and 20 feet

high. The old Tower Hill scaffold once stood in the gardens
of the square. For 400 years, those who lost their heads and
opposed the Crown lost them here for the last time.

To the west stands the church of All Hallows Barking, from
which Samuel Pepys watched the Great Fire of 1666. Down in
the crypt, older by far than the Tower, are fragments of London's roots—a bit of tessellated pavement, Roman masonry and
a Saxon wall about 1,300 years old. The church was gutted by
fire in the Blitz, so that much of the fabric is new, but at the
western end is a Saxon arch dating from about the year 600
and believed to be the oldest in the city.

Beyond, down Byward Street and backing on the river from
Lower Thames Street, lies Billingsgate fish market, rather
smelly and not much to look at except at 6 o'clock in the
morning when it hums in the other sense as well, but opposite
is Lovat Lane, which shouldn't be missed. Its greasy cobbles
lead up to Eastcheap through an old working quarter which
has so far escaped the developers and which provides a suit-
ably maritime setting for the fishermen's church of St. Mary-
at-Hill, a Wren building with a somberly handsome interior.

Sightseers with a passion for altitude may then care to consider the 311 steps to the observation platform of Wren's
nearby Roman Doric Monument to the Great Fire, but the
less energetic will probably prefer the 300-odd paces north-
ward from Eastcheap up Gracechurch Street to Leadenhall
Market. This exuberant, cross-shaped Victorian shopping center under an iron, glass and stone canopy is two stories high
in the middle and bursting with life, plucked poultry and
fish. It stands on the site of the Roman basilica.

On the opposite side of Gracechurch Street, on the corner
of Cornhill, is St. Peter's, another fine church by Wren, but
hemmed in by a cluster of commercial buildings. To see it
best, take the alley opposite the entrance to the Market. This
opens, surprisingly, into a churchyard shaded by two enor-
mously high plane trees. St. Peter-upon-Cornhill is said to have
been founded in A.D. 179, which would make it by far the
oldest church in London.

A little to the west down Cornhill is St. Michael's, designed
by Wren's pupil, Nicholas Hawksmoor, and subsequently
ruined by Victorian improvements. But alongside it is St.
Michael's Alley, a footpath leading apparently nowhere but
in fact to the George and Vulture, a City tavern with an

ancestry traceable back to the 12th century. Before you get
there, however, about half way up the alley, a tunnel to the
left leads out into the tranquil backwater of St. Michael's
churchyard—and the unsuspecting are at once removed from
their present condition. The world has stopped and you have
gotten off. A glass of claret in the Jamaica Wine Bar more
or less opposite the George and Vulture will help to ease the
shock.

From the head of St. Michael's Alley, a few paces to the
right down what is now Castle Court brings up the dark and
sinister entrance to Ball Court. But around the first corner
is the warming presence of Simpsons, among the best of the
City chop houses, whose dark wood, high-backed benches and
polished brass are much as they were when it opened in 1757.

About 200 yards south of here, down Birchin Lane, right
on Lombard Street, then left on Abchurch Lane, crossing King
William Street, you pass St. Mary Abchurch on the right. Turn
then and confront one of the simplest yet most appealing
sights in London.

What was once St. Mary's graveyard is now a pie-slice of
pavement with seats and flower boxes. With its neighbors thus
held back along a diagonal building line, the church presents
its flank to passers-by, a quiet and lovely elevation of dark
brick weathered to purplish brown, stone-dressed, with a
plain doorway and windows in subtly balanced asymmetry.

Wren, of course. No other London architect could have
built a brick barn, pierced it with such easy assurance, added
a simple tower and spire and wrung an answer from the gut
of anyone who cared to use his eyes for the next 300 years. St.
Mary Abchurch is a work of genius, a gentle conception almost
perfectly fulfilled. Inside, he circles the square with a shallow
painted dome, dark in tone though flooded with light, and in
the open space beneath, the woodwork flowers most splendidly under the hand of Grinling Gibbons—the real thing for
once; a tremendous altarpiece and a pulpit top fit to eclipse
an archibishop. There are more important buildings, no doubt,
where Wren aimed higher and achieved no less, but none that
commands more affection.

From the end of the lane, at the corner of Cannon Street,
Martin Lane lies diagonally across to the left on the other side.
It's a short, cobbled street and pleasant enough, but chiefly re-
markable as a setting for the Old Wine Shades, the only City

pub to have survived the Great Fire. Behind its black wooden front, nothing has changed much since 1663. And if its customers have their way, nothing is going to change much in the next three centuries either, although they've got a fight on their hands against developers now threatening for the third time to pull it down. They sip their port where Samuel Pepys sipped his, and that kind of continuity can be comforting. Since the lingering death of English taste sometime in the Forties, the Londoner may no longer know what he likes, but he still likes to know he belongs.

By now, refugees from the tourist assault on the Tower are well ahead of the game. Their easy perambulation around some of the neighborhood's alternative attractions may have taken up the best part of a morning, but it will not have taken them more than a bare half-mile from their original objective. And the time will certainly have been better spent than waiting in line to see the Crown Jewels, which are really rather vulgar.

Around St. Paul's

IF THEY HAVE THE SAME PROBLEM AT ST. PAUL'S, which is quite likely—about four and one half million tourists wear grooves in the steps every year—there's an even richer harvest within a half-mile stroll of the churchyard. (It has to be understood, though, that there is no real substitute for Wren's most thundering achievement; they'll have to brave the grasshopper clicking of Instamatics eventually.) As Ludgate Hill approaches the West Front, one of London's doomed villages, Blackfriars, lies off to the right, sadly reduced by the German air force in 1940/41, as the weedy honeycomb of cellar parking lots still testifies, but with enough remaining higher up the hill to show how a close-knit tangle of streets can lighten the weight of a city by letting people be private.

Not many Londoners live there anymore, but one who does is the Dean of St. Paul's. His house, built in 1670 and one of the few designed by Wren, is set back behind a high wall and gateways with pineapple tops in Dean's Court, the first opening to the right after Ludgate Hill splits on the western prow of the cathedral. If the gates are open, take a quick look inside at the soberly elegant, slightly convex brick front of the Deanery, with its beautiful door case and plane trees roofing the carriage sweep.

Abutting the house on the corner is the old choir school, a disarming relic of mid-Victorian, decorated Italianate architecture which rambles along Carter Lane and now serves as a youth hostel. (The new choir school stands, all too visible, like an assembly of derelict water towers at the eastern end of St. Paul's, opposite the bland, boring and unctuous hulk of the Bank of England extension.)

Carter Lane itself is not especially remarkable, but a little way down from the old choir school between Addle Hill and St. Andrew's Hill, and easily missed, is a narrow foot passage cut through the buildings on the south side. This opens up, most improbably, into Wardrobe Place, a diminutive square, paved and cobbled, with some decent 18th-century brick houses on one side, a few spindly trees in the middle; and opposite, the flank of a long Victorian office building in typical 19th-century, backstairs utilitarian style. But that doesn't matter. The charm of the place is that nobody goes there except to work and mind his own business. Wardrobe Place is an object lesson in how to be private in the middle of eight million people, and being so out of tune with the times, can hardly expect to survive.

From the end of Carter Lane, the view west across the bomb sites and railroad viaduct is instantly seized by the wedding-cake spire of St. Bride's, rocketing out of the muddle of Fleet Street, serene as sugared steel. Wren again. To the left, the cobbles of Black Friars Lane wind down to the yellow-brick front of Apothecaries' Hall, as it turns the corner into Playhouse Yard, presenting an ungiving face to *The Times*'s backside. But the hall's entrance arch gives on to another London oasis, a placid courtyard of late 17th-century buildings, buttered with yellowy stucco a hundred years later. This is one of the few halls of the City's livery companies to have escaped the Blitz, although narrowly—the fires burned out at its doorstep.

Playhouse Yard continues into Ireland Yard, which contains the only fragment remaining above ground of the great Dominican priory that once sprawled over the area, and this in turn leads into St. Andrew's Hill, now, in effect, the village high street. Diagonally across it to the right is a handsome 18th-century rectory adjoining Wren's St. Andrew-by-the-Wardrobe, which is squashed in and difficult to see to its best advantage from the footpath that runs alongside into Wardrobe Terrace. From here, the prospect is blighted by the fearsome ugliness of Faraday House, and the only reason to persevere to the left up Addle Hill to Carter Lane, then right to Godliman Street and so to Knightrider Street on the left is the old Horn Tavern, whence Dickens sent Snodgrass, Tupman and Winkle to buy wine for Mr. Pickwick languishing in Newgate.

To the south, at the corner of Godliman Street and Queen Victoria Street, is the College of Arms, the appropriately noble late-17th-century headquarters of the heralds, set back behind an open courtyard and a pair of very beautiful black and gold 18th-century iron gates presented by an American benefactor in 1956. Under the general direction of the Earl Marshal of England, the College supervises state ceremonial occasions, devises coats of arms, examines the legitimacy of titles and claims to titles and generally attends to all matters of genealogy and heraldry. The three Kings of Arms—Garter, Clarenceux, and Norroy and Ulster—are assisted by the York, Richmond, Windsor, Somerset, Lancaster and Chester Heralds and four Pursuivants, Portcullis, Rouge Dragon, Rouge Croix and Bluemantle—none of whom would seem to have much in common with an age responsible for the bleakly unromantic structures in which office workers are filed like broiler-house hens along the upper reaches of Queen Victoria Street.

Bucklersbury House is perhaps the most graceless, a stolid cliff dwelling stranded on the right above Cannon Street. It is so big and so weak one could almost feel sorry for it. Briefly. The remains of a Roman Mithraic temple uncovered and removed when the foundations were dug in 1954 have been embedded in concrete and set up on a raised platform in the angle of the building. The effect is not unlike that of a village idiot trying to ingratiate itself with the offer of a broken toy.

Around the eastern end, tucked in behind the Mansion House, is Wren's St. Stephen Walbrook, plain to the point of

The City

Leadenhall Market

Cumberland Terrace, Regent's Park

Lovat Lane

Oxford Street

Westway, Notting Hill

Underground

St. George's Gardens

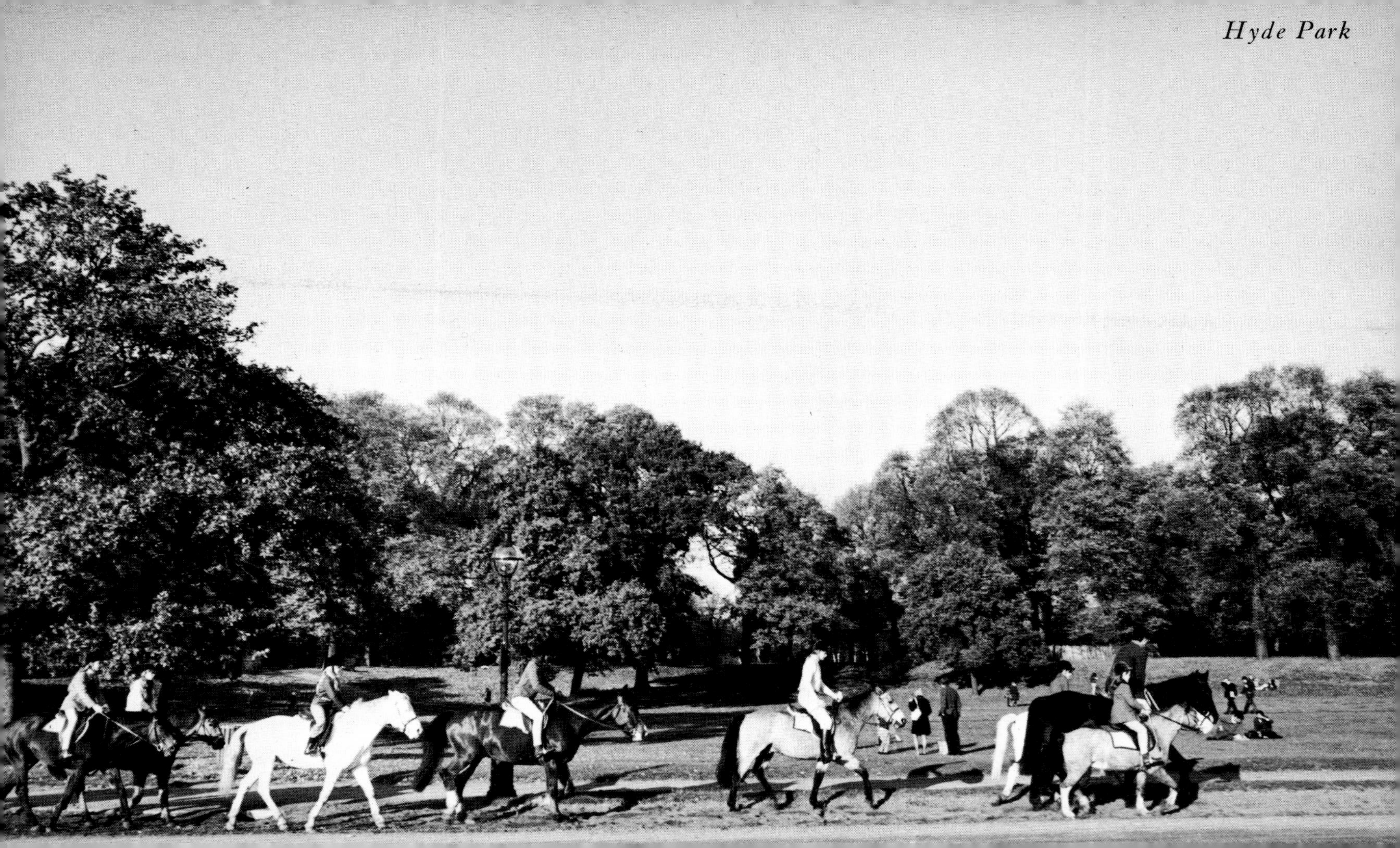
Hyde Park

Kensington Gardens

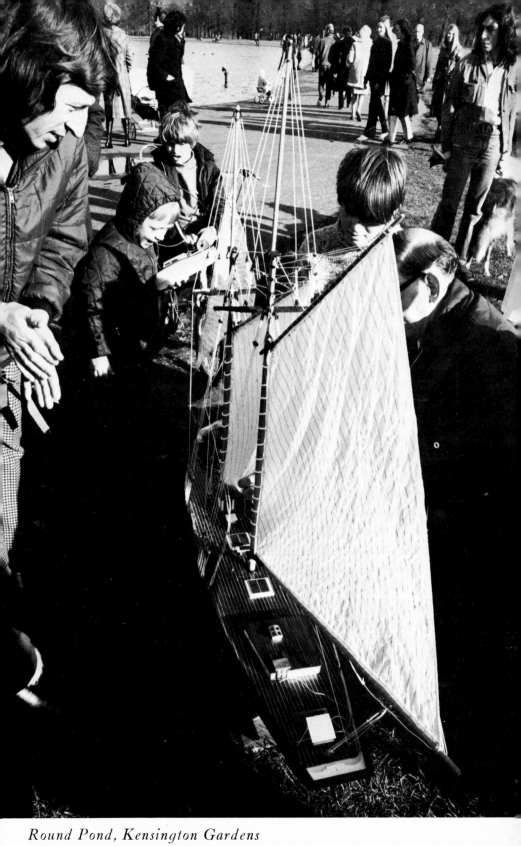

Round Pond, Kensington Gardens

St. Michael's churchyard, Cornhill

Lincoln's Inn Fields

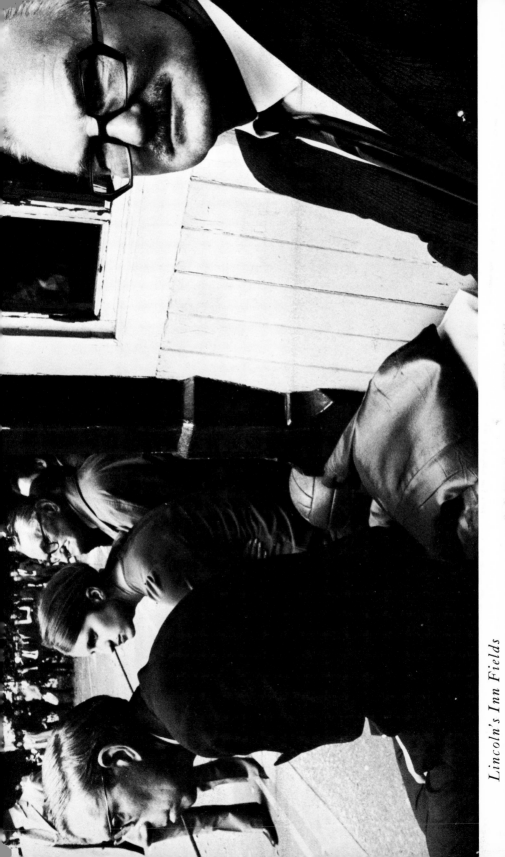

Lincoln's Inn Fields

Performing dog, Lincoln's Inn Fields

primness, a spire and a spare brick box. Steep steps to a
vestibule. Then the coolest flowering of spatial geometry in
London, a stone ballet of Corinthian columns, stationed to a
cross-shaped plan, which order themselves into new combinations with every step and lead the eye up from rectangularity
on the ground to roundness in the dome. Wren built this
church while working on the design for St. Paul's, and it
may well have served as an early model for reconciling the
traditional English church arrangement of nave, chancel and
transepts with a Romanesque central dome. In St. Stephen's,
he not only resolved this conflict but capped the whole brilliant experiment by enclosing it in yet a third kind of church,
the simple, oblong hall then favored by Protestant preachers.

The Mansion House it hides behind is far more imposing
but much less impressive, which goes for all three of the
principal buildings that confront the eight-way intersection at
the end of Queen Victoria Street. The Royal Exchange is the
best, the Bank of England the worst. Passing between the two
up Threadneedle Street, the sightseer in search of something
less commonplace should turn left into Batholomew Lane,
right at Throgmorton Street, which still, on one side, looks
like a sepia print of the City circa 1910, and then immediately
and gratefully turn left into Angel Court, wincing from the
shock of the new Stock Exchange.

And here's another of London's quantum shifts, a perceptible
change of pace and mood just by turning a corner, though the
bowler hats are the same and the buildings quite ordinary,
except for Birch's chop house. These inner courts and alleys
were built for people, not multinational corporations. When
they go—and it's when, not if—the heart of London will die,
like New York's. The City will just be a money machine. But
meanwhile, the top end of Angel Court connects with Copthall
Buildings, a footpath that turns left by a brick-built relic of the
18th-century, narrows and joins up with Telegraph Street. At
this point, a tunnel goes off left through the building opposite
a sandwich bar and brings the sightseer, all unawares, into
Tokenhouse Yard, a bewildering assortment of banks in a no
less bewildering assortment of styles. This leads to Lothbury,
which skirts the rather more appealing derrière of the Bank
of England, and a few paces to the right is Wren's St.
Margaret Lothbury, unpretentious but pleasing and sumptu-
ously endowed with woodwork and furnishings salvaged from

other churches, including a hugely magnificent carved screen.

Lothbury becomes Gresham Street at the junction with Moorgate and Princess Street, and beyond, the first turn to the left is Old Jewry. Visitors, with nerve enough or a foreign accent may care to investigate the handsome secluded court a few yards down from the corner on the right-hand side. And if a tall, uniformed gentleman wants to know what they're up to, they might try asking him for the correct time: it's the headquarters of the City of London police. (Oddly enough, the court is closed on weekends; even crime, it seems, works a five-day week in the City.)

Further down the street on the same side are St. Olave's Court, which is chiefly remarkable for the way in which the tower of Wren's St. Olave's, demolished in the late 19th century, has been grafted onto a small office building, and Frederick's Place, which still preserves some of the distinction the Adam brothers were conferring upon this cobbled yard as the first shots were exchanged at Lexington and Concord.

Poultry becomes Cheapside at the corner of Old Jewry. From here, the church of St. Mary-le-Bow stands about 150 yards to the right on the opposite side of the street. (Halfway there is King Street, with Guildhall at the far end, and tourist buses thick outside.) St. Mary's, the most London of churches, is worth a visit for it most aptly sums up the London condition. It was built by Wren, gutted by the Luftwaffe and restored, externally, with great skill. Rehung in their beautiful tower after 22 years' silence, Bow bells have again been making Cockneys out of every Londoner born within earshot since 1961. From Cheapside, from Bow Lane, from what was formerly the churchyard, all is well, for all is Wren.

The interior, however, is pure Howard Johnson. Nothing more vividly demonstrates the abject poverty of inspiration among British designers and the near-total blindness of their clients. Someone has been at immense pains to make the woodwork look like plastic. The electric chandeliers could only have been obtained in exchange for cigarette coupons. The gold leaf looks cheap. But the crowning touch is a group of gigantic Hummel figures painted in queasy Bavarian pastel shades and suspended from the ceiling. Anxious to be fair, I went back a second time to see if perhaps some subtler merit had escaped me at the first encounter. It hadn't. And before so grotesque an intrusion upon Wren's coolly molded spaces one can only retreat in awe. (The dangling group was a present from the Germans, incidentally. Having failed to destroy St. Mary's in one way, they have now helped the willing English destroy it in another.)

The best corrective, and the best assurance that the world has gone mad, not you, is a glimpse of the real thing. St. Paul's itself is not far away—down Bow Lane, safe at last from developers, first right and there it stands at the end of Watling Street canyon, dark dome and golden ball sailing above the concrete rubbish. But if the buses are still banked up as deep as ever, our energetic sightseer may prefer to wait a little longer and strike north up Foster Lane from Cheapside, past St. Vedast alias Foster with its exquisite spire (Wren again) to Gresham Street and the solid grace of Goldsmiths' Hall at the corner.

Straight ahead is Noble Street, with little St. Anne & St. Agnes set back behind a cheerless open space of brick and concrete. Beyond, at the bottom of a weedy ditch, begins another stretch of Roman wall, a foot or two high, beginning with the outline of a blockhouse and running on until lost beneath the new street called London Wall, which slashes across the southern boundary of the Barbican from Moorgate to Aldersgate.

Spread out here is London's most conspicuous planning failure, a barren affliction expressing ideas of modernity that were outmoded before the work began. As an exercise in urban renewal, the Barbican fails the only tests that matter. It evokes no warmth; no one who lives there could ever think of it fondly. And as townscape it's unspeakable, a desolate, windswept disaster.

The only sensible reaction is an orderly retreat west to Aldersgate. But if it happens to be between 12:30 and 2 p.m. on a weekday, a sally across London Wall and down the steps to the parking lot will find the door open to an underground chamber enclosing the remains of the guardhouse of the Romans' fortified barracks. It's like finding a skull in a hatbox.

Across Aldersgate is the pretty little 18th-century, stuccofronted church of St. Botolph's, which gains in stature with each new atrocity wrought in the neighborhood. And to its left is Postmen's Park, once the churchyard but now a quiet and shady garden with a shelter whose back wall is covered in memorial plaques to ordinary Londoners who lost their lives while saving others. Some are very touching, and one—my favorite—splendidly revealing: "John Cranmer Cambridge. Aged 23. A clerk in the London County Council who was drowned near Ostend whilst saving the life of a stranger *and a foreigner."* (My italics.)

Odd things happen in Postmen's Park. The last time I was there, two elderly ladies were performing some intricate surgery on a pigeon's claw with a pair of manicure scissors. Immensely capable, they seemed rather to resent the occasional advice volunteered by over-anxious bystanders. Indeed, only the patient remained entirely unmoved and eventually flew off, quite unfussed, as if he kept an appointment there with his medical advisers every day.

Nearby, many patients do. At the other end of the park is King Edward Street which, within a few feet to the right, turns into Little Britain and curves around into West Smithfield behind St. Bartholomew's Hospital, better known as Bart's. It is the oldest of London's teaching hospitals, having been founded in 1123, although the present main building, with its splendid gateway to the square, is some 600 years younger than that.

Immediately to the right, as Little Britain joins West Smithfield, is a half-timbered black and white Elizabethan house perched on a 13th-century archway. This leads into the churchyard of St. Bartholomew the Great, which, except for the Chapel of St. John in the Tower, is the oldest surviving church in London—as old, indeed, as the hospital, since both were originally part of the same Augustinian priory.

The gateway is all that remains of the nave of the church; the rest is graveyard. And from just inside, to the left through the railings, is a view of 41 Cloth Fair, arguably the prettiest house in London. Brick and weather-boarded, arched and bayed, it was probably built immediately after the Great Fire, though some think the house may have survived it.

There's nothing pretty about the dark Norman heart of St. Bartholomew's. Though much restored, it bears down with a dead weight of time and masonry. The Tower is hard to take seriously, for all its bulk and bloodshed; perhaps the tourists have tamed it. But nothing has tamed this place, not decay, nor abuse, nor the casual mutilation of other centuries. The church caught the elemental temper of its age, and you can still feel it. Ben Franklin must have felt it, too. He worked here when the 13th-century chapel behind the altar was used as a printing shop.

Blood is another link with the past in Smithfield. Protestants and Catholics burned each other alive here in the 16th century; in the 17th, William Harvey unraveled the mysteries of circulation while working at Bart's, and since the 19th, England's biggest wholesale meat market has occupied the entire north side with its magnificent iron and glass arcades designed by Sir Horace Jones, who also built Leadenhall Market.

Grand Avenue runs through the market from West Smithfield to Charterhouse Street, offering steely perspectives of racks and hooks on both sides. To the right lies Charterhouse Square and Charterhouse itself, once a Carthusian priory and now the home of elderly male pensioners who value their privacy. To the north, about 100 yards outside the half-mile radius from St. Paul's, up St. John Street and then St. John's Lane, is St. John's Gate, all that remains of the priory that the Knights Hospitallers of Jerusalem founded there in 1148, although the gate itself is more recent—about 1504.

To the left, Charterhouse Street runs westward down by the market to Farringdon Road, once the bed of the Fleet River, and then up the opposite bank to Holborn Circus. But before it gets there, a gated entrance on the right, with a porters' lodge, gives onto Ely Place. Go through and you've stepped from London into Cambridgeshire, for this was once the palace of the Bishops of Ely and even now is private ground. No London authority has jurisdiction here, not even the police. Though all that remains of the palace is a late-13th-century chapel to St. Ethelreda, Ely Place still offers sanctuary to the fugitive. No one can be arrested here, not even in the pub, the Old Mitre, which lies hidden in Ely Court, a narrow slot of a foot passage just inside the gate that runs through to London's diamond center in Hatton Garden. Prospective jewel thieves should restrain their enthusiasm, however. The pub closes at 10 p.m. and there are just the two easily guarded exits.

From the south side of Holborn Circus, St. Andrew Street offers almost at once, on the right, an archway through to Thavies Inn, all postwar, shabby and uninteresting. But ahead lies Red Lion Court, with a beautiful house at No. 18, and the usual careless London mixture of periods and styles to Fleet Street. Eastward from here to Ludgate Circus, both sides of the road are honeycombed with courts and passages. The first on the left is Johnson's Court, which threads through to Gough Square, emerging alongside the workaday 17th-century house where Dr. Samuel Johnson lived for 11 years from 1748.

At the other end of the square, a passage runs back south toward Fleet Street, splitting right and left into Hind Court and Bolt Court. The left fork arrives almost at once at a bombsite garden which gives access to Wine Office Court and thus to the Cheshire Cheese, pride and joy of the London Tourist Board. Johnson doubtless frequented the place, though Boswell never mentions it, and on the strength of this presumed endorsement, plus sawdust on the floor and a decent steak-and-kidney pudding, it has become London's number one tourist pub, challenged only by the riverside Prospect of Whitby. Neither is the best of its kind but each serves a purpose, taking some of the pressure off the rest.

Across Fleet Street to the left from Wine Office Court, is Salisbury Court. Before it reaches Salisbury Square, St. Bride's Avenue burrows through the buildings on the left to the front porch of Wren's St. Bride's. Not much more than the tower and spire was left after the Blitz, although you would never know it from the outside. From the inside, however, you would never know it was the same church, although, to be fair, the restoration is marginally less horrific than St. Mary-le-Bow's. No Hummel figures. The real interest, however, is centered in the crypt. This, too, has been made over, in museum supermarket style, but the exhibits somehow survive it, among them a Roman pavement, a tiny Chapel and the foundations of several earlier churches.

St. Bride's Avenue wriggles around the church to Bride Lane, passing on the corner the Old Bell Tavern, which is as old as the Cheshire Cheese—1667—though much less famous. And Bride Lane, in turn, wriggles away to the right to New Bridge Street, which has nothing to offer apart from the decorous Georgian façade of the Bridewell Hospital offices at number 14 and the *art nouveau* opulence of the Black Friar pub on the corner of Queen Victoria Street. Its heavily decorated interior, the best of its kind in London, has been known to detain sightseers until closing time, especially after this circumnavigation of St. Paul's.

Around the British

THE HALF-MILE AROUND THE BRITISH MUSEUM offers leaner pickings. Poor Bloomsbury. Poor Holborn. What was once a well-aired, mainly Georgian precinct of real, if not outstanding, quality has been ground down to the point of disintegration by neglect, greed and philistinism. Local government allowed parts of it literally to collapse on the sidewalk, as on Millman Street. Private developers made their usual contributions toward the destruction of neighborhood quality. But worst of all, because the least excusable, a massive onslaught has been made by the very institution that should have been most jealous of Bloomsbury's character—the University of London. Its ruthless carving up of Bedford Way, Gordon, Woburn and Torrington Squares has been cited in extenuation of all kinds of barbarism, lending much aid and comfort to the enemy. But enough remains to remind us of what has been lost.

South of Great Russell Street and the Museum is a huddle of small streets full of bookstores, curio and print shops, tenements, pubs, coffee bars and other places of refreshment, including the handsomest pizza joint in town. It is a friendly neighborhood of charm, character and utility—so naturally the planners would like to pull it down. The space is needed, they say, for new Museum buildings and to open up a view of its frontage from New Oxford Street and Bloomsbury Way. But not everybody feels that the architecture of the Museum is worthy of so great a sacrifice—it is, indeed, a very large but rather dull building—and critics of the plan eventually managed to enlist the borough council on their side, thereby winning a temporary reprieve. The final decision will depend on the outcome of a duel still going on between government and council planners, and the longer it lasts the better the chances of victory for the conservationists. Public opinion is slowly coming around to their side.

At its eastern end, Great Russell Street runs across the top of Bloomsbury Square, third in order of seniority of London squares but now chiefly remarkable for its underground parking lot and a fine corner building with a pilastered stucco façade built by Nash around 1777 for the Pharmaceutical Society. Some better inkling of what Bloomsbury was once all about is offered by Bedford Place, which runs north from here to link up with Russell Square. It is a spacious, comfortable street of brick and stucco dating from the late 18th century and astonishingly well preserved.

Which is more than can be said for Russell Square. Indeed, the less said about it the better. A few decent houses survive and the gardens are accessible and pleasant, but everything else is abominable; one of its nastier hotels, for instance, artfully tricked out in gold and orange and blue mosaic tiles, could only be cured with dynamite.

A right turn at Southampton Row, then a left into the foot passage of Cosmo Place brings up Queen Square, full of hospitals except for a sprinkling of Georgian houses on the west side. There are more of these on Great Ormond Street, both before and after it crosses Lambs Conduit Street, and more again as a right turn at the end into crumbling Millman Street leads onto Great James Street. This is the northern extension of Bedford Row, the two being separated by Theobalds Road, and both are nearly complete Georgian streets of fine quality.

Further east along Theobalds Road, opposite the silky lawns and noble planes of Gray's Inn, there's another one, John Street, which soon turns into Doughty Street, circa 1790, where, at No. 48, Charles Dickens wrote "Oliver Twist" and "Nicholas Nickleby." It is the only one of his London homes still standing.

Crossing Guilford Street, Doughty Street runs into Mecklenburgh Square, the east side of which, facing the gardens, is a rather splendid setpiece by Joseph Kay built in 1812. And now comes another, typically odd London happening. A left turn on Heathcote Street leads to St. George's Gardens, an old cemetery turned into a public park. And very handsome it is too, with its serpentine paths winding between lawns and flower beds and tombs. On a fine day, one can sit on a bench under a tree, listen to the shift of the leaves in the cool, never-quite-still London air, read the headstones propped against the wall and meditate upon the transience of life. Others go there to eat their sandwiches. It's a strange place—a figment of someone's imagination—a movie set.

The gate at the western end leads into Handel Street, which crosses Hunter Street and then founders on the fringe of a municipal housing project conceived in the style of the "new brutalism." Except that the architects were too soft hearted. The project no doubt represents a net increment of toilet bowls and modern plumbing, but the only evident brutality has been done to the feeling of neighborhood. The buildings themselves are simply another compromise thrashed out in committee, though mercifully lower than most.

A right turn on Hunter Street, then left on Tavistock Place restores some sense of community. Now there are comfortable old shops and people going about their business; the scale is human again and adapted to use; it's a living cell, surviving, precariously, in the shadow of cost-efficiency. From March-mont Street, Cartwright Gardens, once Burton Crescent, curves smoothly away to the left; late Georgian this, quite plain and full of cheap hotels, but shaming most else in the neighborhood. Halfway around, Burton Place cuts back into Burton Street, where a right turn and a left leads to another jewel in a base metal setting—Woburn Walk, a perfectly preserved little street of three-story stuccoed houses and shop fronts built by Thomas Cubitt in 1822. It is one of the best-mannered bits of urban design left in London, and, luckily, protected against all comers. Even the people are better-looking around here. They belong to The Place, a theater and school of modern dance around the corner on Duke's Road, which runs down past the improbable Greek-revival church of New St. Pancras to join the traffic millrace of Euston Road.

At the other end of Woburn Walk is Woburn Place, and across the street, diagonally to the left, is Tavistock Square, the first of a sequence of squares designed and built with complete assurance by Cubitt and the Sims between 1820 and 1860 and subsequently mutilated, with complete indifference, by London University—Tavistock Square (only the west side façade remains), Gordon Square (east side), Woburn Square (nearly all gone, except for the much altered Warburg and Courtauld Institutes on the northwest corner), Torrington Square (a fragment only), and thus to Byng Place, Torrington Place and the corner of Gower Street.

When a one-way, northbound traffic system was introduced for Tottenham Court Road in the Sixties, Gower Street, a long, straight, broad avenue lined on its west side by a pleasant enough terrace of blackened Georgian brick houses, became both the southbound route and the best drag-racing strip in town. The biggest casualty was Bedford Square, about a quarter of a mile down from here. Though perhaps not of the highest quality, it is easily the best preserved and most complete late-18th-century square in central London, and while the damburst of traffic that now floods across its eastern end may have left its fabric unimpaired (so far), it has completely exploded the mood of mock-rural seclusion the square was built to enclose.

A hundred yards more and Great Russell Street cuts across what is now Bloomsbury Street, and the railings of the British Museum are a little way up on the left.

Around Trafalgar Square

THE HALF-MILE AROUND TRAFALGAR SQUARE and the National Gallery offers more richly exhausting possibilities. To the northeast, there's all of Covent Garden for a start, though not for much longer. It's the last quarter in central London still free from developers' blight, but the bulldozers are waiting in the wings, and it seems certain to go the way of Les Halles. Meanwhile, try approaching it from Charing Cross Road through Cecil Court, or St. Martin's Court, Goodwin's Court (if you can find it—the enchanting row of 18th-century shopfronts are worth the effort), New Row and King Street.

The fruit, vegetable and flower market is squashed in between the Opera House at the eastern end and Inigo Jones's St. Paul's in the west to make a marvelous, ramshackle sandwich of art, commerce and decayed religion, liberally garnished with tenements, restaurants, theaters, studios, pokey offices, pubs, publishers and one-man businesses of every kind. For most of the day, and a good part of the night, it's stuffed with produce and pandemonium, but the market is worked in, lived in, used and enjoyed more thoroughly than probably any place else in the city. So of course it had to go. When the market moves out in 1973 to the site being prepared for it on the south bank of the river at Nine Elms, the developers are due to move in. What exactly they mean to do with it is not yet decided; various plans have been put forward, attacked, modified and attacked again. But whatever the final decision may be, it is clearly only a matter of time before the patient dies under surgery, some well-intentioned, some not.

Nobody expects miracles. Covent Garden is neither a museum piece nor one of the world's architectural wonders, though there are good things in it. Embalmed by the conservationists, the Garden would no doubt die just as surely. But London more than most cities would profit greatly from a moratorium on urban renewal until the planners learn how to do it—or at least until architects and their clients recognize a higher imperative than achieving maximum floor space at minimum cost.

An early example of how not to do it can be found on the opposite side of the Strand from Covent Garden in the pitiful remnants of the Adam brothers' Adelphi. Some notion of what it was all about can be seen by looking east up John Adam Street, with the Royal Society of Arts on the left and the elegantly proportioned façade of No. 7 Adam Street, the only survivor with the original decorative treatment, closing the view. And that's about all. The improvers began to tamper with the Adelphi's ordered magnificence in 1872—about 100 years after work began there—and finished it off in 1937 by demolishing the great central terrace overlooking the river to make room for the whey-faced hulk of the Shell-Mex building, a direct ancestor of the postwar Shell Center which now performs a similar disservice for the South Bank. Wring what consolation you can from Buckingham Street, and its fine old houses, some with door hoods, which run parallel with Villiers Street down to a watergate, once at the river's edge and now on the lip of Victoria Embankment Gardens.

South and southwest of the National Gallery are virtually all the set-piece vistas in London, except from the river. She is not a grand city, given to expansive public gestures in the manner of Paris or Washington. Such urban landscaping as she does possess exists by courtesy of the Crown, a few of the great London estates, one or two brilliant planners—notably Nash— but chiefly by accident.

The view down Whitehall from the steps of the National Gallery itself isn't bad, particularly on a fine day with the fountains raining on the square. And for a cramped city, there's a pleasant spaciousness to the broad reach of the Mall, ruler-straight and tree-lined from Admiralty Arch to Buckingham Palace. To stand at the northern tip of St. James's Park, with one's back to the Citadel blockhouse and the two-tiered white back-drop of Carlton House Terrace colonnading on down to the right, is to understand how lucky London was in a monarchy that liked its capital well-ventilated. London is generally at her formal best when pretending not to be a city at all—an affectation that Nash well understood and expressed to its best advantage from the bridge across St. James's Park lake, the view toward the minarets of Whitehall being quite properly celebrated as one of the most romantic in Europe. The ducks ride lower in the water here than anywhere else in London. They are so pampered they'll only eat cake.

On the other side of the Mall, a more distinctly urban pleasure can be taken in St. James's Palace. There are some imposing buildings within its precincts—indeed, the palace it-self, in red Tudor brick, is made to seem almost humble in the massive presence of Marlborough House, Lancaster House, Clarence House and Bridgewater House—but there is nothing really grand about the cumulative effect. It's all rather cozy and domestic, with courtyards and streets and passages quietly wandering about to fill in the corner between Green Park and the Mall. It's only when you start reading the nameplates on the grace-and-favor apartments that you realize this isn't exactly the hub of British democracy.

Back on St. James's Street, still maintaining a vaguely resi-dential air because of its clubs, the 18th century again re-proaches the 20th in the absurdly picturesque shopfronts of Lock's, the hatters, and Berry Bros. & Rudd, wine merchants.

Less familiar, and approached through a passage immediately
to the left of Berry Bros., is Pickering Place, four brick
buildings of about the same age arranged around an irregular
court with three claims to fame. The last duel in London is
said to have been fought here, Emma Hamilton rented one of
the houses and the short-lived Republic of Texas chose it as
the site of its embassy (ambassadors still present their letters
of credence at the palace across the road). Less quaint and
a good deal more lively is Crown Passage, diving through
from Pall Mall to King Street and cutting off the corner.
Bristling with sandwich bars and very un-West End shops, it
caters to the backstairs life of the now rather seedy gentility of
St. James's.

Relics of its former glory still survive in St. James's Square,
however, notably on the west side in a splendid 18th-century
town house by James Stuart for the Earls of Lichfield, now occupied by the Clerical, Medical and General Life Insurance
Company, and on the north side in the somber dignity of
Chatham House, numbers 9 and 10, where three Prime Minis-
ters, Pitt the Elder, Lord Derby and Gladstone, lived, and
which now, fittingly enough, accommodates the Royal Institute of International Affairs. But for the most part, this the
senior of London's squares has been butchered as carelessly
over the years as Berkeley and Hanover Squares, though the
gardens help redeem it in spring.

To the north, Duke of York Street runs up past the cut-glass
glitter of the Red Lion to Jermyn Street and the parish church
of St. James's, Wren's favorite but not mine, although I see
what he meant. I often wish I had known it before it was
bombed, before the usual inelegant touches were added in the
course of restoration. The light fixtures, for instance, would
make better sense in a bus depot.

To the east of the square, the main function of Charles II
Street is to focus the sight lines on the brilliant cream façade
of Nash's Haymarket Theatre, a composition that improves
beyond the traffic trench of Lower Regent Street, which itself
provides a decent view south to Waterloo Place, where the
Duke of York on his pedestal surveys St. James's Park. Then,
just before the Victorian fuss and frilliness of Her Majesty's
Theatre on the Haymarket corner, Nash strikes again, off to
the right with the Royal Opera Arcade to Pall Mall. Less obvious and less famous than Burlington or Piccadilly Arcades, it

is also cooler and prettier to my mind, the effect not at all
spoiled by a second row of shops chiseled into the backside of
New Zealand House. Across the Haymarket, Pall Mall East
allows a sideways glance up Nash's Suffolk Street, all balance
and composure, before joining the northwest corner of Trafalgar Square.

Due north from here is Leicester Square, where the starlings
live and young suburbia lets its hair down on Saturday nights,
and beyond, still within the half-mile limit, lies much of Soho,
seething with waiters, strippers and customers. By day, it is
raffishly domestic—42nd Street crossed with the Village; by
night, full of mystery and of lurid promise, dire and delightful,
that is somehow never quite realized.

To the south, the Whitehall half-mile curves gently down
through basic tourist territory to Parliament Square and the
Abbey, too well-beaten a path to need much signposting,
although sightseers would be well advised to spend a little
less time photographing Cousin Effie with a Life Guard and
a little more on Inigo Jones's Banqueting House across the
street. It was the first classical building in London, and still
arguably the best. Not even the cheap brass chandeliers and
its bare shabbiness can diminish the nobility of this room or
the full-blown Rubens ceiling. Commissioned by Charles I in
1630, it was the last agreeable thing he saw before confronting
his executioners on the scaffold outside.

Around Westminster Abbey

WESTMINSTER HALL AND WESTMINSTER ABBEY will also be
crowded. Like the Tower, St. Paul's, the British Museum and
the National Gallery, they shouldn't be missed, but they can
be postponed. If the sightseer reaches the Abbey at lunchtime
and skips a guided tour, half an hour will give him something
to think about. If he wants to go back another day, or another

year, it will still be there—which is more than can be said for some of London's humbler attractions. And there are plenty of these within a half-mile of the Abbey, including the not-so-humble Tate Gallery.

Immediately to the south is one of the best preserved bits of early Georgian London, a snug little nest for rich Members of Parliament almost within earshot of the division bell. Four discreet streets of blackened brick terraces, all neat, trim and proper and dating from about 1720, run from Gt. College Street through to Smith Square, where, on the north side, a row of slightly younger houses, perhaps 1726, confront Thomas Archer's startling Baroque church of St. John, begun in 1713 and recently restored after war damage. The best sequence to follow is up Barton Street, left as it becomes Cowley Street, across Great Peter Street into Lord North Street, right in Smith Square and back down Gayfere Street to Great Peter Street again. And you may meet Mary Poppins on the way.

Great Peter Street leads to the no-man's-land of Marsham Street. With one of those apparently unconscious ironies that happen so often in London they begin to seem sinister, the Ministry of the Environment, charged among other things with the protection of Britain's architectural heritage, recently moved into three enormous glass slabs on Marsham Street of such consuming dreariness that one might be tempted to see them as the ultimate affront to a long-suffering city if not morally certain of still worse to come. There is one picture postcard view of London that everybody knows—Big Ben and the Houses of Parliament from the South Bank, all fretted and spiky and sailing serene on the chop of the Thames. No more. Hang on to your postcards. The Ministry of the Environment has turned them into collectors' items.

Marsham Street connects with Horseferry Road, which heads west toward Pimlico. As it angles right at Regency Place, Maunsel Street goes off to the left between pretty little tarted-up terraces to Vincent Square, unexpectedly large, low-rimmed and very quiet except when the boys of Westminster School are out on the playing fields. From here on, it's late Victorian London trying to house the new middle class without giving it ideas above its station, but then suddenly there's Westminster Cathedral, headquarters of the Roman Catholic Church in Britain, crouching like a dinosaur with its tremendous striped neck of a campanile craning over the tenement rooftops. The still unfinished interior is very impressive, though perhaps becoming less so as multi-colored marble creeps up to cover the rough brick walls.

A few yards further on is Victoria Street, whose emetic qualities are superior even to those of Marsham Street. Flight is the only solution, back toward the Abbey then left at Palmer Street, more or less opposite the Army & Navy Stores, to find sanctuary in another old foot passage with shops and a bit of color and humanity about it.

This crosses Caxton Street by Caxton Hall, where pop stars and fashionable divorcees posture on the steps for their wedding pictures, and so to Petty France. A right turn here, then a left, brings up Queen Anne's Gate, a well-preserved street of early-18th-century houses, very mellow and urbane, with some nice porches and a statue of Queen Anne which has stood there since 1714. As the far end bears left into Old Queen Street, Cockpit Steps curl down to Birdcage Walk at a point near the southeast corner of St. James's Park, offering placid views through the trees toward the bird sanctuary and Horse Guards. From here, it is just a few hundred yards back to Parliament Square.

Around Buckingham Palace

WITHIN HALF A MILE OF BUCKINGHAM PALACE lies the southern fringe of Mayfair, a thick slice of Belgravia and much of Victoria—a 180-degree sector from north to west to south. (The eastern semicircle takes in territory already covered by half-mile sweeps from the Abbey and National Gallery.) Most of this is familiar territory; indeed, the only surprise left in south Mayfair is that so much of its 18th-century fabric still survives. Not that it isn't threatened. In 1974, most of the Shepherd Market leases fall due, and already there is talk of redevelopment (a term that begins to evoke as much dread in London hearts as parking meter or Common Market).

The best way to approach it from the palace is across Green Park to Whitehorse Street, scarcely 400 yards of grass and trees, yet so subtly contoured they cheat the eye into thinking Piccadilly twice as far away. Whitehorse Street leads into the Shepherd Market place, now reduced to a single fruit and vegetable barrow, and beyond lies a warren of streets and alleys full of tourists by day, venturing cautiously down from the Hilton to see if the natives are friendly, and of loiterers by night, carrying rolled-up newspapers and hungering for a glimpse of the Naomis, Myrtles and Chloes whose doors stand so invitingly ajar.

There's a decent pub, the Grapes, which serves one of the better cold buffet lunches in London, and a pleasant oyster bar, Embersons, which is so restful you wonder how they stay in business, but everything else is synthetic—a couple of quaint tourist restaurants for the homesick from Red Neck, N.J., some quaint tourist shops for the last-minute gift trade and a plush gambling casino on Hertford Street for disposing of surplus travelers' checks. The Hilton, now joined by Londonderry House and the Inn on the Park, and with the Bunny and Penthouse Clubs both within spitting distance, has brought a kind of international anonymity to this section of Mayfair, which must be comforting for those who like to feel they've been to London without actually having had anything to do with it.

Park Lane, a broad river of southbound traffic, pours past the Hilton into the maelstrom of Hyde Park Corner. At prodigious expense and inconvenience, the planners constructed an underpass between Piccadilly and Knightsbridge in the early Sixties which transferred part of the traffic jam a hundred yards to the west, but the effect, if any, on rush-hour congestion has long since worn off. One of London's lesser known tourist attractions is to stand in the calm green eye of the storm—if you can work out how to get there through the labyrinth of underground walkways—and watch staid British breadwinners heading for home in their family sedans turn suddenly into kamikaze pilots as they enter Hyde Park Corner and revert as abruptly to type upon leaving it.

On the north side stands the Duke of Wellington's Apsley House, No. 1 London, austere and a little forbidding but well worth a visit to see some of his loot from the Peninsular Wars, including three Velasquez. To the west is St. George's Hospital, a rather nice stucco building of 1827, and Grosvenor Crescent, which swings down to the petrified splendors of Belgrave Square, much of which is now foreign territory as only embassies can afford the rent. Designed by Basevi in 1825, the general effect is immensely grand, but it is only on the broad streets leading off the square, like Belgrave Place, that anyone below the rank of duke, say, could feel at home, and then perhaps only if he were an earl.

Built to last by the Cubitts, Belgravia was London's final great fling in the Georgian classical tradition. First to cross Belgrave Place is Eaton Place, all cream-stucco opulence; then Eccleston Mews to the left and Eaton Mews South, meant for coachmen and servants but now more highly prized (and priced) than the apartments into which most of the great terraced houses have been divided; next, Eaton Square, triple carriageways spaced by long belts of garden with high terraces on either side screened by trees and shrubbery; then Eaton Mews South, domestic again but still chic, and thus to Chester Square, with a density of resident Americans about equal to Manhattan's upper East Side.

After that, there's just Ebury Mews before Ebury Street surrenders to the proximity of Victoria Station in a welter of shops, flats, offices and bed-and-breakfast hotels. A left turn here leads into the station-approach traffic of Grosvenor Gardens and across to Beeston Place on the other side, with Lower Grosvenor Place and the wall of the Royal Mews closing the end. Just off to the right, though, is Victoria Square, a delicate Georgian rebuke to the elephantiasis of Portland House on the other side of Buckingham Palace Road. The palace now lies a few hundred yards down on the left, past the Queen's Gallery, where she graciously teases her subjects with glimpses of the most valuable private art collection in the world.

If he has stayed the course, the determined sightseer may now be in danger of thinking he knows London. Probably he has seen as much of her as most Londoners, who tend to commute between home and office and end up seeing nothing, but in fact he has done little more than be formally introduced. And as in any courtship, the main business begins once the preliminaries are over.

At this stage, the suitor of London has only the sketchiest idea even of her physical charms. He has yet to take a stroll through the country from Westminster to Notting Hill, for instance, with grass underfoot all the way except for the four streets he must cross in three miles. He has still to wander through the Inns of Court, from the Embankment to Holborn; the law, being a rich profession not noticeably dedicated to efficiency, refuses to budge, thank God, from its 800-year cross-section of the best in London townscape. He has yet to confront her from the river, her principal thoroughfare for the first 1,600 years and still the best way to Hampton Court or Greenwich. He hasn't caught her facing the wrong way on a narrow boat voyage on the Regent's Canal.

Southwark, Bankside and the whole of south London are still a closed book. So is the civilized calm of the Georgian streets, terraces and mews north of Wigmore and Seymour Streets; not outstanding, perhaps, taken building by building —except for odd treasures like Robert Adam's Chandos House on Chandos Street—but wonderfully consoling nevertheless after all the shopping-bag bashing on Oxford Street. Then there's the jerrybuilt charm and low-life vitality of Bayswater, Paddington and Notting Hill Gate. He hasn't heard the peacocks screech in the woods of Holland Park. Or peacocks of another kind braying at each other in the richer pastures of Knightsbridge, Kensington and Chelsea as the West End moves further west and the air comes alive with the rustle and scent of new money.

So far, he knows nothing of the crumbling East End and its amiable hustlers. He has yet to see the trendy slums of Islington and Camden Town, all broken out in bright paint and carriage lamps as the middle class reclaims them. The gentility of St. John's Wood, the smugness of Hampstead and Highgate, the preciosity of Primrose Hill are still a mystery to him.

Above all, he has yet to catch London at her most supremely theatrical. Of all the works of John Nash, none are more brazenly artful than his Regent's Park extravaganzas. Cumberland and Chester Terraces are the most spectacular. Like all great dramatic performances, they are best seen —particularly for the first time—at night, with an orange-lit sky for a backcloth and street lamps painting them with creamy gloss and shadow. Approached from the Zoo across open ground, they show themselves little by little between the trees until finally all is revealed, a coolly fantastical vista of giant colonnades and porticos, triumphal arches, screens, courtyards and pavilions, a huge pediment writhing with ample matrons in white relief on Wedgwood blue, heroic statuary posturing on the roof—a brilliant spectacle unmatched in London or anywhere else.

But even then, like all of London's suitors, he will find she still eludes him. There's simply no knowing her in any *final* sense; she confounds every judgment with endless exceptions to the rule. Diverse as the people who built her, she is the aggregate of their experience; all her suitors can do in the end is take her as she comes—and be thankful.

Chapter Six

. . . the inn place

NEVER MIND about the Mother of Parliaments, cucumber sandwiches and the role of sterling as a reserve currency—the one unequivocal boon the English have conferred upon a suffering humanity is the London pub, an infinitely subtle instrument for reconciling man with society, financed by the sale of beer, wine and spirits between officially designated licensing hours.

Dr. Samuel Johnson, who made a close study of the subject, once observed that "there is nothing which has yet been contrived by man by which so much happiness is produced as by a good tavern or inn." If he was right (and who would dare dispute it?), London should be the happiest place on earth. She has over 7,000 taverns or inns, catering to every mood and occasion, every nuance of social grouping, every trade, profession and vocational interest, every taste in decor, theme and atmosphere, and practically every appetite for diversion permitted by a fairly permissive society.

Londoners go to pubs for solitude and company, for a cheerful noise and a bit of peace and quiet. They go to meet a friend or find one, to play games or watch them, to sing, to dance, to talk, to get something to eat, to solve the problems of the world or forget them, to heckle a drag queen, hear a poet, watch a play, listen to jazz or walk the dog. Some even go to drink. But most of all, they go to pubs to belong, to have a place and find a welcome. And because they can't do so whenever they feel like it, there's always a sense of occasion when the doors open at 11 or 11:30 a.m. (till 3 p.m.) and 5 or 5:30 p.m. (till 11 p.m.) (That's on weekdays. On Sundays, the times are 12 noon till 2 p.m. and 7 p.m. till 10:30.)

There are huge pubs and tiny pubs, chic pubs and vulgar pubs, country pubs and city pubs. There are Tudor pubs and

Stuart pubs, Georgian pubs, Victorian pubs and very nasty new pubs. Not to mention folk pubs, rock pubs, sporting pubs and river pubs; pop pubs, gay pubs, hippie pubs and drag pubs; lawyers' pubs, doctors' pubs, writers' pubs, business pubs, theater pubs, travelers' pubs and unself-conscious pubby pubs. Nobody alive could fail to find a second home in a London "local," and there is no more pleasurable aim in life than setting out in search of it.

Those planning to spend less than about five years on the quest, however, must necessarily simplify matters with a sampling operation known as "the pub crawl." The derivation of this term is uncertain, but it could have something to do with the means of locomotion to which unwary tourists are sometimes reduced at the end of an evening's injudicious sampling of pub hospitality. A precautionary word about English beer and etiquette may therefore be in order.

In the main, English brewers are not what they were when the Rev. Sidney Smith was moved to exclaim, "What two ideas are more inseparable than Beer and Britannia!," but they still make their American counterparts look like soft-drink manufacturers. Strong and full-bodied, London beer comes in 11 main varieties, five draft (served in half-pints and pints) and six bottled.

Without doubt, the greatest of these is draft bitter, a clear amber beer strongly flavored with hops and drawn from a wooden barrel. Connoisseurs are bitterly divided (so to speak) as to the merits of rival brews and, as most pubs are owned by breweries and tied to their products, generally allow their palates to dictate the choice of local. (Youngs and Fullers are widely held to be the best of the London beers.) Next among the drafts is keg bitter, drawn from a pressurized metal canister and easier to keep in good condition but scorned by the knowledgeable; then mild ale, darker and sweeter than bitter, with which it is sometimes mixed; draft Guinness, a creamy black stout now found in many of the best pubs, and finally draft lager, which is gaining ground and comes closest to American beer, though still somewhat stronger.

The bottled beers offer rough equivalents to the drafts and a few more besides. Light or pale ales correspond to bitter, though weaker and fizzier, and brown ale to mild. Then there are bottled stouts and lagers; export ales, stronger than lights, and barley wine, which comes in small bottles and packs a wallop like whisky.

All of these, draft or bottled, will be served with the smallest possible head on them. Unlike his American cousin, the British beer drinker is not fond of dipping his nose in froth, and instantly suspects a short measure. He's paying for beer, not bubbles. And with rare exceptions, all 11 varieties will be served at ambient cellar or bar temperatures. Before alienating the natives by adding ice, therefore, which is an un-British activity, the tourist owes it to himself and his national honor to try a half-pint of best bitter, slowly and thoughtfully, giving his palate a chance to respond after years of carbonated abuse.

If the verdict still goes against it, never mind; some people still prefer coffee to tea. There yet remains a whole world of liquid refreshment to explore: lemonade or ginger beer shandies (beer plus soft-drink mixers), cider (bottled or draft and decidedly alcoholic), lager and lime, simple mixed drinks (gin and blackcurrant is mystifyingly popular), wines and fortified wines like sherry and port, cordials (liqueurs to the British), a good assortment of spirits, with 100 or more brands of Scotch whisky to compensate for the virtual absence of bourbon and rye, soft drinks, fruit juices—indeed, an armory of thirst-quenchers as various as the places to sample them in.

The one thing it is not safe to order is a cocktail, especially a martini. This is to court embarrassment or worse, for nobody knows how to mix one. To insist on a whisky sour, for instance, will not only endanger the health but also, at 10 minutes before "Time, gentlemen, please," imperil London's otherwise deserved reputation for courtesy.

Nor is it safe to rap on the bar, wave money, snap your fingers or interrupt a barmaid's conversation; she will get to you eventually. You are in *her* house and the only permissible method of attracting attention is to look thirsty. As tips are not accepted, you cannot *buy* her favor, although she may allow you to buy her a drink if she likes the look of you and is not too busy. (The one exception to the no-tipping rule is in a few pretentious pubs where drinks may be served in the lounge bar by someone waiting on tables.)

The only other points to remember are that nobody under

the age of 16 is allowed in the bars, although they can go in the garden if the pub has one, and that in quiet old-fashioned pubs, tourists may feel more comfortable in the saloon or lounge bars than in the public or private bars, where the regulars usually congregate. There will be less of a pause and a turning of heads upon entry.

All that now remains is to decide where to start. With more than 7,000 pubs scattered over 700 square miles, no London pub crawl can offer more than an arbitrary sampling. And even with a car (and a driver who sticks to ginger ale), it will be difficult to do justice to more than three or four per midday or evening session. The best plan, therefore, is to set out hopefully with a few pubs in mind, no fixed schedule and a readiness to let whim and impulse take care of the rest.

A good place for tourists to start is the Red Lion on Waverton Street, Mayfair. It's a nice old country-style pub of the sort British Travel publicity has made familiar, with beams and settles and horse brasses and the dolliest barmaids in town. Jammed at lunchtime with deafening young advertising executives slopping beer and gravy over each other, it calms down at night into the kind of amiable sophistication which London achieves at her easy-going best.

Less sure of itself and its customers is The Audley, at 43 Mount Street. Awarded the puzzling title of The Most English Pub in Mayfair by the American Hotel Federation in 1960, it was recently remodeled to provide a late-Victorian extravaganza of a Buffet Bar, all gilt and velvet on the street floor; a joke-Victorian fish and chip shop on the floor above, and in the cellar a bar called The Gilded Cage for swinging young bloods and their birds. Despite an impressive collection of bric-a-brac, the result is more like a movie set than a period interior, but those who prefer instant antiquity to the slow-percolated kind will find no better example in London. The buffet lunch is also very good—although an even finer one can be had not far away at the Grapes in Shepherd Market, particularly when there's an "r" in the month and oysters are in season.

The best piece of *authentic* Victoriana in the neighborhood is on the south side of Piccadilly, on Duke of York Street; another Red Lion, but this time a cut-glass brilliant, a varnished jewel of a night-time pub where customers should wear stiff collars and Derby hats or high-button shoes and feather boas and watch themselves refracted to infinity in flashing mirrors.

The Salisbury, in St. Martin's Lane, is a bigger, blowzier, warmer-hearted version of it, an opulence of glass and brass, varnish and plush, exploding at night with a smoky glitter and road of talk as the crush of bodies against the bar ebbs and flows with the rise and fall of theater curtains. It's an actors' pub, larger than life, with a lunchtime matinee, starring a buffet like a harvest festival.

The same expansiveness of mood invests the Lamb & Flag on Rose Street, Covent Garden—a bare 200 yards away but back another 300 years in time. Licensed in the reign of the first Elizabeth, the pub gloriously hams up its own history; never was there such a gallimaufry of blackened beams and dimpled glass, plates and earthenware and pewter mugs and prints and writings on the wall (including a price list for the local "jilts, cracks, prostitutes, night-walkers, whores, she-friends, kind-women and others of the Linen-Lifting Tribe)."

Known as "The Bucket of Blood" when bare-knuckle prize-fights were held upstairs, the pub bridges the tunnel-like entrance to Lazenby Court, a dark alley which needs only a touch of sulfur fog to prompt thoughts of Jack the Ripper. On the roof of the tunnel, the bewhiskered landlord of the Lamb & Flag, Bernard Nelson Bessunger, apostrophizes the passing trade with this hand-painted legend:

"STAY TRAVELLER, rest and refresh thyself in this Ancient Tavern, within whose walls so many great figures of the past have taken their ease. Here often sat the immortal Charles Dickens and his Friends, poor Samuel Butler and the wits and gallants of the Restoration. Hither resorted the Bucks and Dandies to witness prize-fights and cock-mains, while hard by was enacted the notorious Rose Alley Ambuscade in December, 1679, when the poet Dryden was almost done to death at the instance of Louise de Keroualle, Mistress of Charles II."

This last, dastardly incident is commemorated each December 19, when Mr. Bessunger invites a group of regulars and celebrities, who have included the likes of Peter O'Toole and Maria Callas, to dine on roast suckling pig and listen to poetry readings upstairs in the Dryden Room. Downstairs, the Landlord "difpenfes a Glafs of Sack Pofset or Mull'd Ale to all prefent without charge; This is called Dryden Night, & all interefted Perfoms are requefted to inquire for an invitation."

No one should wait for an invitation at any other time of year; the Lamb & Flag serves the best game pie in London.

Atmosphere of another kind is provided by The Sherlock Holmes at 10 Northumberland Street, a "theme" pub of little interest except for its collection of Holmesian artifacts and memorabilia. Standing on the site of the Northumberland Hotel, where Sir Henry Baskerville stayed, it offers a replica of Holmes's Baker Street study in the upstairs restaurant, recreated just as Sir Arthur Conan Doyle described it, right down to the "VR" in bullet holes in the wall. Patrons dine there under the glassy eye of the dummy with which Holmes outwitted Moriarty's Colonel Moran, and drink there in the basilisk gaze of the Hound of the Baskervilles, whose fearsome head surveys the downstairs bar. Other mementoes of Holmes's famous cases include the cobra from "The Speckled Band," pistols, handcuffs and plaster footprint casts.

Nobody could pretend that these six pubs are the best in the West End or even a particularly representative cross-section, although each is good of its kind. There are hundreds to choose from, and pub-crawlers soon develop their own standards of judgment. None can be written off on sight, for even the worst of the Muzak-and-plastic horrors inflicted on flagging pubs by misguided brewers in the course of "modernization" can sometimes be redeemed by the people who use them.

On the other hand, most West End houses suffer from a mild schizophrenia which in the eyes of the cognoscenti prevent their ever quite achieving the ultimate heights of pubdom. The essence of a great local is its steady trade, the regulars who live in the neighborhood and use it as an extension of their living rooms. The gossip is about one another, the atmosphere domestic. Strangers are welcome, within reason, but they are left in no doubt as to whose pub it is. Stepping into the Saloon Bar of a good local in a residential area is rather like joining a ship in mid-cruise: the passengers all know one other and share a common bond of experience—it is their cruise. In the same way, a pub belongs to its regulars.

The closest most West End pubs can get to this is at lunchtime, when they do a lively trade with people working nearby, but in the evening, with few exceptions, their customers tend to be as anonymous as a railroad station's. To catch a truer flavor of pub life, it is necessary to go farther afield—downriver from Bankside, let's say.

From here to its estuary, the Thames, as a working-class river, bred working-class pubs, for watermen, dockers and sailors. From Bankside and Southwark to Rotherhithe, then back up on the north bank through Wapping and the City to Blackfriars, they are spaced out like pearls in a necklace of crumbling brick; bright, narrow-hipped houses wedged in between the fortress hulks of gaunt Victorian warehouses.

They are pubs in transition. As the Port of London's traffic ebbed away downstream, so much of their traditional trade went with it. But now business is picking up again as their dwindling quorum of regulars is reinforced by Londoners rediscovering the special magic of Thameside taverns, that powerfully romantic blend of booze and history, of warmth within and river chill outside, of lights and movement on the water and a huge sky.

Bankside is a good place to start (and this is a pub-crawl which *has* to be motorized; the distances are too great for comfort on foot and public transport is not of much help). Practically all that remains of the pleasure grounds that once stretched west from London Bridge along the southern bank is The Anchor, at the corner of Bankside and Bankend. Shakespeare, Burbage and company probably used the tavern that stood on this site as their local, for the Globe Theatre was a mere 200 yards away, but both went up in smoke in the great fire of Southwark in 1676.

The present Anchor was built about 100 years later, and at once renewed its literary associations, becoming yet another of Dr. Johnson's favorite haunts. Like Charles Dickens a century later, Johnson must have had a tankard in his hand as often as a pen. Between them, they seem to have drunk in as many pubs as the first Queen Elizabeth slept in four-poster beds. But certainly Johnson went often enough to The Anchor with his friend Mrs. Thrale for both to have rooms named after them there.

On one side of the tavern stood the Clink jail—of which only the name survives today in the common expression "in the clink" for in prison—and on the other· side, the great

brewhouse founded by James Monger in the reign of Elizabeth and operated today by the John Courage Brewery, the
Anchor's landlord. It is said that Johnson was much addicted
to the tavern's Imperial Russian Stout, made next door
especially for Catherine the Great of Russia and still brewed
there to the same potent recipe 200 years later. What is more
certain is that Johnson, while acting as Mrs. Thrale's executor,
auctioned off the brewery with these immortal words: "I am
not selling a parcel of boilers and vats—but the potentiality
of growing rich beyond the dreams of avarice."

Though barely two centuries old, The Anchor has taken on
the aura and associations of a more remote past. It is a
rambling wood-framed building on many levels, with low
ceilings, paneled or beam-and-plaster walls and uneven floors.
There are secrets in this house. Upstairs, on the restaurant
level, is a paneled room with a handsome bay window. Before
recent alterations, it had five doors, three giving access to
the room from various parts of the house and two opening
on to huge closets. At the back of one was another door, and
behind it, an apparently solid brick wall. No satisfactory
explanation for this has yet been advanced.

Nor is there an answer to the riddle of the shaft, large
enough to hold a man, which runs vertically through the
middle of the house from the first floor to a skylight on the
roof. Access can be had through a panel in the shaft to a
room with a window but no door. Was this a river pirate's
hide-out? A smuggler's lair? A sanctuary for fugitives from
the Clink?

A glass or two of Imperial Russian Stout may encourage
wilder theories.

Inland from London Bridge, off the east side of Borough
High Street, Southwark, is The George. This is not a river
pub at all, but an Elizabethan coaching inn of such formidable
charm that any excuse will serve for a visit. Built around
a cobbled center courtyard, of which only one galleried side
remains, it is in fact a 1677 replica of the original George,
which had burned down, like the Anchor and most else in
Southwark, the year before. No other galleried inn survives
in London, which is one good reason why it now belongs to
The National Trust. Lovingly described by Dickens in "Little
Dorrit," The George has enlarged its literary reputation in

recent years by staging occasional summer productions of Shakespeare in the courtyard.

Of the three entrances, one leads to the taproom and bar, hung with pewter mugs; another to a pair of dining rooms, furnished like a City chophouse with high-backed settles, and a third to the twisting staircase which leads up to the galleried bedrooms, double-decked, like a Mississippi steamboat. Nobody stays at The George anymore, but a lot of people go there for its traditional English cooking.

Downstream from here, and not far apart, are a pair of classic riverside pubs on Rotherhithe Street, the Angel and the Mayflower. Built on piles in the 16th century, the Angel, with its balcony overhanging the water, is perhaps the better known—thanks partly to Samuel Pepys and, more recently, to the fashionable young photographer Anthony Armstrong-Jones, who kept a studio nearby before being translated to another, more regal sphere by way of marriage to Princess Margaret—but the Mayflower is perhaps the better pub.

Its setting is more romantic, for starters, squashed in between two warehouses in a tiny Georgian precinct dominated by Rotherhithe Church, a robustly handsome building which screens it from a dismal hinterland. But what must surely clinch the pub's place in American affections is that the Mayflower was fitted out nearby for its voyage to the New World and set sail from the adjacent steps to pick up its Quaker passengers at Plymouth. (Another trans-Atlantic link is the pub's unique license to sell both American and British postage stamps, a privilege granted originally as a convenience for sailors but now of more interest to tourists.)

The house, originally 16th-century, is heavily beamed, with a bar downstairs and a pleasant restaurant above it overlooking the river, the whole decorated with bits of armor, weapons, prints and old documents. But the Mayflower's principal attraction is its veranda, reached through the Saloon Bar and jutting out over the brown river between brown buildings hung with ropes and hoists and watermen's paraphernalia.

The Thames is peaceful but never still, and here you get a sense of involvement with it, with new laws of motion, a different scale of view, new ratios of sky to earth to water. The wind is fresher. River craft slip by, intent upon their silent business. Huge, blunt barges grind restlessly against each other, tugging at their cables, the empty ones booming now and then like the slamming of steel doors. The Mayflower's veranda is a window on another kind of life striking unsuspectedly through the middle of our own.

Evening is the best time for a visit, with London turning on a virtuoso sunset, one of those soundless explosions of red and gold that linger for an hour, fading off through all the shades of heraldry till clouds of plum and lavender are banked against a green sky. The river blackens into oil. The low rim of warehouses on the far bank darkens to a cliff, except for the twinkling Prospect of Whitby across to the right.

The driest way over is by the Rotherhithe Tunnel. Though debatably the most famous pub in London, the Prospect of Whitby is also one of the hardest to find. People living nearby are so used to motorists asking for directions that they generally start describing how to get there before your window is fully wound down. Built in the reign of Henry VIII, the pub is worth a passing visit, although not for any insight it is likely to provide into London life. Often on a summer evening, the only English spoken there is by the barmen— not that it really matters because there is usually a Hawaiian or West Indian or local rock group playing in the bar and conversation is impossible anyway. It was no doubt quieter in Whistler's day when he painted the river views from the terrace.

The next stop along the north bank, heading back now towards central London, is the Town of Ramsgate, a genuine local on Wapping High Street which visitors either miss or deliberately pass by on their way to and from the Prospect. A narrow, 17th-century house favored by river policemen as they come off duty from their headquarters nearby, it rates high in atmosphere and low in extroversion. Fishing boats from the Kent port of Ramsgate used to unload at Wapping Old Stairs and it was here that hanging Judge Jeffreys was captured by the mob while trying to escape from London disguised as a sailor.

On past the Tower, the square-mile City of London has just two pubs overlooking the water, both new: the River Side at Southwark Bridge to show how not to do it and the

Samuel Pepys at Brooks Wharf, off Upper Thames Street, to restore some faith in the virtue of brewers.

The Pepys is a riverside "theme" pub which opened in 1968 in a gaunt Victorian citadel of a warehouse due south of St. Paul's. And given the general insensitivity of modern British design, it is remarkable for its intelligent use of traditional materials and relative restraint. The architects have steered a very creditable course between the plastic Scylla and cute Charybdis to find a nice blend of ancient history and modern heating.

Downstairs in the stone-flagged Chandlers' Bar, some trouble has been taken to preserve the warehouse feeling, in honor of Pepys's role as Secretary to the Admiralty. The bar is decorated with the signs and wares of merchants who supplied and provisioned the Royal Navy in the 17th century. Claustrophobics may feel happier in the Pepys Bar upstairs, however, which has a veranda with stirring views up-river and down.

Sandwiched between them is a restaurant which, the designers say, is intended to symbolize Pepys's amatory exploits. The tables are set in curtained alcoves named after the inns at which he entertained his mistresses, and five of them (tables, not mistresses) are arranged in a facsimile four-poster bed. Intriguing though this may sound, those planning to dine there on the pub's Olde English Fare are better advised to make a reservation in the window than in bed.

The Pepys is not a true local, however, because nobody lives nearby to provide a hard-core regular trade. The same applies to the Black Friar at the foot of Blackfriars Bridge —indeed, this isn't a river pub either, but it falls conveniently at the end of a westbound riverside crawl and, like the George on the other bank, is not to be missed by anyone in the vicinity during licensing hours.

Though not much to look at from the outside, apart from some luscious detailing—it is shaped like a generous piece of cake and apparently props up one end of the railroad bridge across Queen Victoria Street—the Black Friar has an authentic *art nouveau* interior unlike any other in London. (The meat and fish hall in Harrod's is an even finer example, but they won't let you sit down with a half of bitter to admire it.)

Picking up the neighborhood associations with the Dominican priory that once straggled all over the south slope of Ludgate Hill, rotund friars in copper relief on marble direct little homilies at the customers: "Industry is all," "Haste is slow." The landlord is rather less censorious, encouraging the sin of gluttony at lunchtime with a lavish buffet in the barrel-vaulted snack bar at the back.

In the evenings, there is a flurry of business as office workers making for Blackfriars Station across the road stop off for a quick one before catching their trains to suburbia and that's it—the trade has gone with them, out of the commercial into the residential districts, where the real locals are.

Though scarcely a typical suburb, Belgravia is very convenient for the visiting student of pub sociology, and his increasingly knowledgable eye will have little difficulty in assessing the quality of The Grenadier in Wilton Row. If he can find it. For this is mews territory, the servants' quarters, deliberately hidden away.

Wilton Row begins as a slot between two buildings at the eastern end of Wilton Crescent and winds back behind it, going nowhere, littered with Rolls's and Maseratis. Then just as you are about to give up, vowing never to trust another guide book, and thread your way back through all this expensive machinery, there it is around the corner—plain, unimproved and reeking of class in one of the most appealing pub locations in London.

This is the heartland of the deb and her chinless wonder, though, to be fair, the breed has improved a lot since P. G. Wodehouse. Earning a living tends to stiffen the spine. They have also been joined in force by the socially upward-striving, and as each tends now to affect the speech and manners of the other, it becomes increasingly difficult to tell the genuinely overprivileged from those who, for perverse reasons of their own, simply like to be thought so.

Not that the distinction is of much value or any importance but the litmus test of what used to be known quaintly as "good breeding" is self-assurance. Whereas the striver is always very conscious of others and the effect he is having on them, his beau ideal is totally oblivous of everyone he is not actually speaking to. Just as well-born ladies taking tea in

Speakers' Corner

Lincoln's Inn Fields

Revivalists, Hyde Park

The Serpentine

Regent's Park

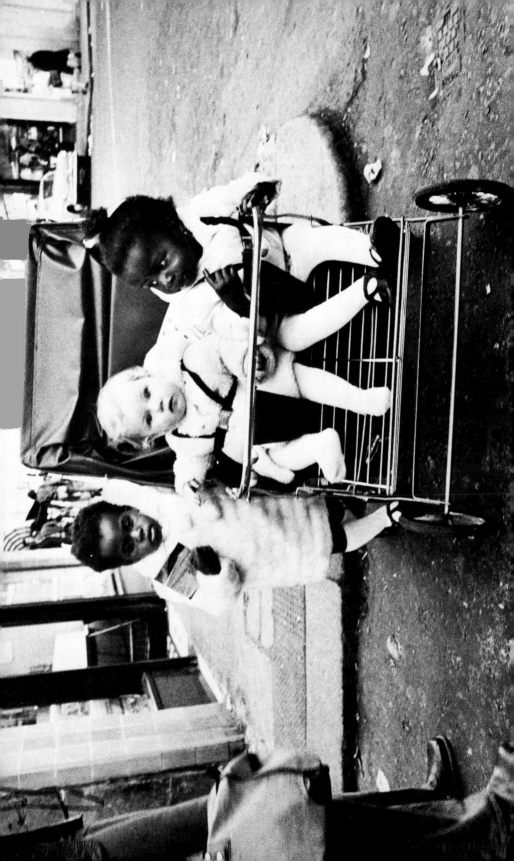

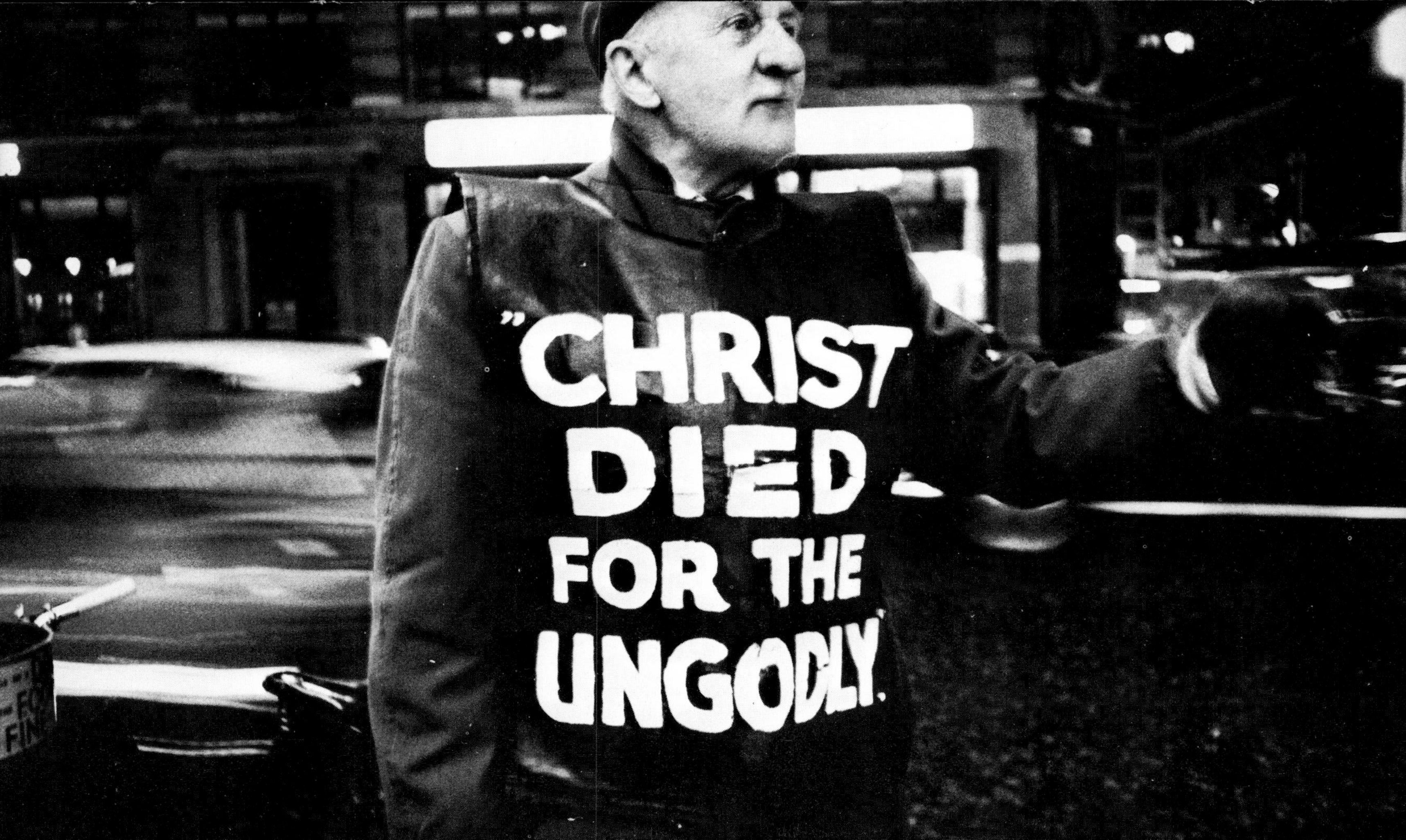
"CHRIST DIED FOR THE UNGODLY."

Totters—One of London's mobile junk dealers

Organ grinder, Notting Hill

the Soda Fountain at Fortnum & Mason literally see no reason to lower their voices, so does the Eton-Sandhurst-Guards insurance underwriter chatting up his Roedean doxy at The Grenadier utterly fail to realize he is blocking the way to the bar.

And what a nice bar it is—comfortably shabby, like a good piece of well-used furniture. Anywhere else in London, with all this money around, they would have installed plastic beams, wall-to-wall carpets and horse brasses long ago. But here, somebody had sense enough to realize that The Grenadier stands in the same relation to a West End transients' pub like the Audley as, say, the Junior Carlton Club does to the Westbury Hotel.

The army associations are kept up, without being labored, by a collection of prints and bits and pieces of militaria, and the ceiling is plastered with wine labels. Apart from this, and the fact that the barmen wear mess jackets, the decor is amiably unobtrusive, heightening the mood of sociability without eliciting "oohs" or "ahs" or "ughs." And the Duke of Wellington is said to have played whist there.

Belgravia is full of good, tucked-away pubs, as any gentle meander through its cream-stucco ravines will demonstrate. Down on the southwestern corner by Sloane Square, for instance, is The Antelope at 22 Eaton Terrace, an elegant Victorian house that happily survived a recent facelift without much loss of character. Though not quite in the same league as The Grenadier, it suffers less from the plague of beautiful people, and some will prefer it on that account. On the other hand, it is often taken over by Belgravia's beer-swilling hearties, and the dominant impression left after half an hour in *their* company is a sharp headache. The most peaceful time for a visit is generally at midday, when the alcoved dining room upstairs can provide a tolerable lunch.

West of here, along the King's Road, the hearties thin out and the trendies take over, together with their sub-species and hangers-on. Caught in the middle, the Chelsea Potter deserved a better fate than the one that overtook it when the neighborhood became the epicenter of Swinging London—although the landlord probably didn't mind as the place has been jammed to the doors ever since. And to do him credit, he hasn't lowered his standards, even though his customers would have been too busy admiring themselves to notice. It remains a comfortable brown blend of Victorian and modern, the food tastes as if it were cooked instead of defrosted, and he still serves about 40 different wines by the glass. Keeping up with the exotic tastes of his clientele, he can even cope with demands for tequila, arak and sake.

A bit farther down the road, opposite Chelsea Town Hall, another old pub called the Lord Nelson wasn't so lucky. It recently met its Waterloo in a trendy reincarnation called the Trafalgar. This is a rather extreme example of a disturbing trend among major brewers, Bass Charrington in this instance, not only to cut the ground from under their own feet but also to undermine the guiding principle of pub development since the days of the Saxon alehouse. The Trafalgar is not really a pub at all. It's a discothèque open between licensing hours—and what's more, a discothèque passing itself off as a funfair.

Customers sit in dodgem cars around a dance floor and the bar has been tricked out as a carousel. Strobe lighting flickers over a decor of high-voltage red, orange, pink and yellow, relieved only by splashy murals and bar fronts with funfair or circus motifs.

The intention, according to the brewers, was to produce "a cheerful and relaxed habitat which they hope will appeal to the discerning and fashion-conscious clientele of London's most fashionable street." Whether or not their hopes have been realized is hard to say—"relaxed" is a curious adjective to employ in such a context—but the logic of this redevelopment remains obscure.

There are people who like going to pubs, others who like going to discothèques and still others who like going to funfairs. Indeed, it is even possible to find people who like going to all three—but surely not all at the same time. Neither pub nor disco, and certainly no funfair, the Trafalgar set out to be with-it and wound up without it. Confirming everybody's worst fears about contemporary British interior design, it is worth a look if only to teach one not to waste any more time on modern pubs. (But, needless to say, it is packed every night.)

Useful antidotes are Finch's on the Fulham Road, darkly Victorian and vaguely Irish in feeling, with its heavy woods and beer puddles on the bar top; the magnificent 19th-century bourgeois assurance and dolly barmaids of The Bunch of Grapes on Brompton Road, one of the best pubs in London (but let's try to keep it to ourselves), and the dazzling crystal palace of Paxton's Head on Knightsbridge, a glazier's tribute to the designers of the Great Exhibition of 1851 held just down the road in Hyde Park.

Perhaps the most extravagant contrast, however, would be to try one of London's country pubs. There aren't many left now and they are too far apart for any ordinary pub-crawl but most of them are worth an expedition in themselves. They are survivors of the first great wave of improvements that broke over London's village fringe in the last century. And while the Victorians were probably better modernizers, on balance, than their successors—there being a certain integrity, at least, about varnished wood and etched glass—the sad fact remains that hundreds of honest rural pubs were fed into the maw of urban progress to emerge with improved lavatories but impaired characters. (Just how subjective the notion of progress can be is rather nicely illustrated by today's nervous brewers who are now reworking many of their outlying pubs to capture in plastic a conception of pastoral England that never existed outside of Disneyland.)

The pubs that managed to escape the wheel of fashion without serious interference are generally to be found near the outer ring of London parks. Two of the best and most accessible are in Highgate and Hampstead—The Flask and The Spaniards Inn. Compared with the urban pub, they offer not merely a shifting of gears into an easier cruising speed but a positive difference in quality. They have a holiday feel; you have journeyed out of town.

The Flask, at the top of Highgate West Hill, is a picture postcard pub, built in 1663 around one corner of a village green and substantially rebuilt in 1716. To sit outside on a bench of a fine summer evening with a pint of beer and somebody agreeable to talk to is one of London's quieter pleasures, even though the village green is now hardly more than a parking lot for the customers' Jaguars. On weekends and most evenings, The Flask gets pretty crowded but the temper of the place is such that there is no disturbing sense of having to compete for space and attention; the crush at the bar is good-natured—all will be served in the end. Robert Rodgers stayed here in 1765 to draw up proposals for the land route to the Northwest Passage, and William Hogarth was so impressed by a fellow customer's lopsided expression (after he had punched him in the jaw) that he painted him into "The Rake's Progress."

The Spaniards Inn on Hampstead Heath is perhaps less attractive superficially in its plain white cement and weather-boarding but is truer to type and in the end probably more satisfying because of it. Besides, it has one of the best pub gardens in all of London (somewhat improbably, Dickens had Mrs. Bardell convene her tea party there in "Pickwick Papers"). Winter or summer, Sunday noon is the best time to come upon it, preferably after a windy walk across the Heath from Hampstead village.

In winter, dogs sleepily singe their bellies before the open fires and the shadowy yellow light glistens on plaster and paneling glossed ochre and black with age and smoke. Tensed against the cold outside, newcomers quickly thaw out in the pub's enfolding cheerfulness—it's a good place to be in rough weather. Or when it's fine, come to that. In summer, the rambling bar-rooms are dark and cool as caves, and their comfortable indoor smell of beer and food is laced then with garden-scented air.

It's not hard to understand why The Spaniards has counted among its regulars Goldsmith, Byron, Keats, Shelley, Sir Joshua Reynolds, Lamb, Leigh Hunt and sundry less peaceable gentlemen of the road, including Dick Turpin, England's answer to Jesse James. There have been many dark and violent deeds upon the Heath. The muskets on the wall in the saloon bar, for instance, were taken from a party of Gordon Rioters disarmed at the inn on their way to sack and burn Kenwood House, then the home of Lord Mansfield, further along the road toward Highgate. In these less turbu-lent times, visitors to Kenwood House have nothing more sinister in mind than dropping candy wrappers in Robert Adam's splendid interiors or listening to an outdoor concert down by the lily-covered lake.

Music of a different kind is provided by another great category of London locals—the entertainment pub. A bit of a boozy sing-song accompanied by one of the lads bashing away at a beer-sodden upright piano with sticking keys is not uncommon in working-class pubs on Saturday nights, but the landlords of many of them have ventured into show-

biz in a thoroughly businesslike way over the last 10 years.
Some have climbed on the rock bandwagon; others have
turned to jazz and folk, booking professional acts and even
advertising coming attractions in their local papers.

More significant, perhaps, reports of the death of variety—
the English version of vaudeville—have turned out to be
highly exaggerated. Off-stage, the stand-up comics, singers
and entertainers of the old days could usually be found in
the pubs; now they're working there, too—especially in the
East End. Anybody interested in finding out whatever became of English music hall can spend a delightfully rowdy
evening pub-crawling around dockland between the Iron
Bridge Tavern, the City Arms and the Waterman's Arms
getting his susceptibilities scorched. Londoners always were
a bawdy lot behind their conventional hypocrisies. Today,
with fewer notions of respectability to restrain them, the
patter, jokes and innuendo are liable to curl a Boston lady's
hair at 40 paces. Particularly as they will more than likely be
delivered by transvestites.

Not that female impersonation is any new thing on the
British stage. Sexual ambiguity is a long, if not quite honorable, tradition—particularly in children's entertainment.
Christmas pantomimes like "Dick Whittington" and "Puss in
Boots," for instance, always feature a Principal Boy, who is,
in fact, a girl; and comic relief from a Dame, who is, just as
naturally, a man. After the usual vicissitudes, true love invariably triumphs. Principal Boy gets Principal Girl and off
they go, hand in hand and without so much as a raised eye-
brow, into a Lesbian sunset. With no psychiatrists to nag
them about it, generations of primly brought up children—
and their parents—have accepted all this without a moment's
misgiving, which may help to explain why there is nothing
particularly epicene about the audiences at East End drag
shows. At the Iron Bridge Tavern, for instance, the customers
are mostly longshoremen and truck drivers out for a giggle
with their aggressively normal wives or girlfriends.

One has to be a little more careful at The Black Cap in
Camden Town, however. On Saturday nights, there are liable
to be as many potential drag queens at the bar as there are
actual ones on stage. The working-class audience has here
been thoroughly infiltrated by middle-class trendies descend-

ing from the intellectual heights of nearby Primrose Hill to refresh themselves among the common people for an hour or two before closing time.

At 11 o'clock, 7,000 London publicans are calling, "Time, gentlemen, please," in increasingly sterner tones. The Mayfair, Belgravia and Kensington pubs empty out to brays of well-bred laughter and car doors slamming like gunfire. Outside the Irish pubs of Kilburn, there'll be a little bit of scuffling, perhaps, as departing groups of suddenly bosom friends lurch into each other on the sidewalk. And down by the docks, the girls can't stop giggling in the parking lots.

Arthur Prout and his missus are saying good night to their regulars at The Widow's Son in Bow. Some member of his family has done so every night for 139 years. This mercifully unimproved late-Georgian pub is named after the widow's son who wrote home saying his ship was due to dock on Good Friday and would she save him a hot cross bun. The ship never docked and that was the last the widow ever heard of him, but every year until she died she added another bun to the collection—a custom continued to this day by all the landlords of the pub built on the site of her house. Though some of the very oldest buns were shaken to dust by the bombs which laid most of this area waste during the war, the rest still hang in a blackened mass over the bar.

This lovely pub is hard to find and will soon be gone forever, pulled down as part of a street-widening project. The vandals are in the saddle, and we can only hope the spirit behind The Widow's Son and all the other lovely pubs that offer a truce twice daily in the wear and tear of city life is less easily destroyed.

At The Lamb & Flag in Covent Garden, a 14th-century Latin toast is inscribed on two beams over the bar. As freely translated by Eric Linklater, it reads:.

> *"This is what I now propose:*
> *In a tavern I shall die*
> *With a glass up to my nose*
> *And God's angels standing by*
> *That they may indeed declare*
> *As I take my final tot*
> *May God receive with loving care*
> *Such a decent drunken sot."*

Amen to that. The pub is the greatest of British inventions, and in them you will find the truest expression of national virtue. Hilaire Belloc thought so too. "When you have lost your inns," he wrote, "drown your empty selves, for you will have lost the last of England."

Chapter Seven
. . . a night errant

*I*T DEPENDS on what you mean by a night out, of course. London's fleshpots are as comprehensive as her cultural facilities, and no less accommodating. In either department, no taste is too obvious or too rarefied, no whim too prosaic or fanciful. She is cerebral and vacuous, frugal and gluttonous, prim and debauched—a place where the lamb and the lecher can lie down together yet keep their illusions intact. Whatever you like to do can be done in London, and it's almost bound to be cheaper.

Three people, for instance, sometimes four, can sit in the best seats of a London theater for the price of one in New York, and at much shorter notice—unless, of course, it happens to be the National Theatre Company you want to see, in which case now would be a good time to book for next year. The best plan, if theater-going is high on the agenda, is to write ahead for prospectuses and postal booking forms from the National and The Royal Shakespeare Company. Having settled the heavyweight division in advance, you can sort out the middle and lightweight contenders on arrival but do it early. *Time Out* is fairly reliable in its assessments of current productions, and if you can't take time out to buy the tickets, have the hotel porter or an agency do it for you. Everything they say about the London theater is true. There are 48 houses, plus theater clubs, offering anything from matinee moonshine to social subversion. Something startling is usually going on somewhere, so see what's playing at the Royal Court and its Theatre Upstairs, the Jeanette Cochrane, the Mercury, the Round House, the Open Space and the Greenwich Theatre. But if it's the National or nothing, try corrupting a British fan with a want ad in the Personal column of *The Times* offering to buy his tickets at three or four times what he paid for them. If it works, you'll give *him* the pleasure of confirming his deepest suspicions about American imperialism and yourself the pleasure of the National's company at no more than customary New York prices.

The London musical scene is, if anything, even more lavishly endowed. Five of the world's great symphony orchestras are quartered there—the London Philharmonic, the New Philharmonia, the Royal Philharmonic, the London Symphony and the BBC Symphony—and two of its finest chamber orchestras, the English Chamber Orchestra and the London Mozart Players. These riches are matched by an equal wealth of front-rank instrumental groups, choirs, bands and soloists, and augmented by a year-round procession of visiting musicians, so that on any given evening, there'll be a half-dozen or more concerts and recitals to choose from—not counting opera or ballet at the Royal Opera House, Covent Garden, or by the Sadlers Wells Company at the Coliseum. Listings for the week ahead can be found in *Time Out* and in *The Times* on Saturday mornings.

There is no season. In fact, the world's greatest musical orgy takes place in London during the summer. The Henry Wood Promenade Concerts, founded in 1895 and now sponsored by the BBC, run six nights a week, plus some Sunday afternoons, from mid-July to mid-September at the Royal Albert Hall. Upward of 15 orchestras, 30 conductors, 20 choirs, 60 instrumental soloists and 100 singers, all of international repute, work their way through a schedule of 50 or more concerts, drawing enthusiastic audiences of up to 7,000 people a night. Nothing quite like it happens anywhere else, and no visiting concert-goer can afford to miss out on this ultimate musical festival—especially at Prom prices. The most expensive seat in the house is $3. (Try for Block H.) Promenaders get in for 85 cents. (The Arena is more fun, but the Gallery has more room.) And for musical gluttons, a season ticket—for 50 concerts by the world's leading performers—costs under $20.

If that isn't enough, there's a South Bank Summer Music Festival during August at the Royal Festival Hall, free band concerts every evening in Victoria Embankment Gardens, rain or shine, from mid-May to September, and a series of Hollywood Bowl-type open-air concerts in the grounds of

Kenwood House in June and July (admission 50 cents, or 75 cents if you insist on a deck chair). Keep an eye open for recitals and chamber music concerts in the Victoria and Albert Museum and in the gilded halls of the City of London livery companies, which are not otherwise open to the public. And when you've spent all your money, don't forget that free tickets for broadcast concerts are generally available from the BBC Ticket Unit.

You can sometimes get to hear jazz that way, too, although the BBC is not so strong in this department. True fanatics will camp out for as long as they can afford it at the Ronnie Scott Club in Soho, where they are sure to hear the best around, or at the 100 Club on Oxford Street, bastion of the traditional, New Orleans school (though purists prefer the Colyer Club). But most of the action these days is in the jazz pubs, like the Bull's Head on the river at Barnes, the Tally Ho at Kentish Town, Merlin's Cave in Finsbury (Sundays at noon) and the Phoenix in Cavendish Square (Wednesday nights). The ubiquitous *Time Out* again covers the ground pretty thoroughly, but the final authorities on the London jazz scene can be found every weekday serving their customers at Collet's Record Shop on New Oxford Street and at Dobell's fantastic record store on Charing Cross Road.

They'll be decidedly sniffy, however, about pop, rock, reggae and all the other mutants favored by ravers at places like The Marquee, Hatchett's, Tiffany's and Bumpers. These are easy to get into. Membership discothèques can be harder, sometimes impossible, although a display of passports and travelers' checks often helps. If you are rich and insistent, try Annabel's or Tramp; if less rich but persistent, you may carry the day at The Saddle Room, Speakeasy or Bag o' Nails. If rejected everywhere, you can always fall back on a bout of lost-generation nostalgia at New York prices in the old-line nightclubs. There's no problem about instant membership at the Astor, Churchill's, the Embassy or the 21 Club, provided you're wearing a tie. They'll even supply someone for a small fee (say £5—$12.50) to help drink your champagne (at, say, £7—$17.50—a bottle).

But rich visitors often prefer to throw their money away in casinos, and here the rules are much stricter. There's a minimum 48-hour waiting period for membership, so gamblers should check in on their arrival in town—at the Clermont Club, if you're very rich and they'll have you, otherwise at Curzon House or Crockford's. And if none of these like the look of you, there's always the Palm Beach or the International Sporting Club to fall back on and, in a pinch, the Playboy Club or the Victoria Sporting Club, who'll take almost anybody. The games are all honest, and why not? In 1970, the Playboy Club's gambling profits amounted to £1,750,000—about $4¼ million.

The casinos—some 20 of them in London—are, in fact, very strictly policed by the Gaming Board, which has the power to close any one of them down for quite minor infringements of the rules. It put the illustrious Crockford's out of business for no worse a crime than employing Algerian managers, and permitted the club to reopen only when ownership had passed into British hands—a lesson not lost on would-be Mafia infiltrators. There are no Vegas-style cabarets to lure the suckers in, credit is hard to come by, and only milk, coffee and soft drinks can be served at the tables, although there is reason to believe that the coffee cups of big players sometimes harbor something stronger. The general intention is to see that losers have no one to blame but their own sober, willing selves.

On the whole, American gamblers are not much admired. Too emotional. Too addicted to dice. Arabs and Greeks are preferred because they never argue with croupiers and take their medicine like lambs. Baccarat is *the* game, although everything else is available, including poker, blackjack and *punto banco*. Chemin de fer is fading away, although you would never think so at the AM Casino where £3 million a year cross its five tables. Elsewhere, beginners might start to get the feel of things with roulette. London's one-zero wheels halve the odds that favor the bank in Las Vegas. As against that, being free to fix their own limits, the casinos usually set minimum and maximum stakes at a ratio that makes it tough for losers to get back, and tough for winners to get ahead. As tipping is not allowed, they also sew up their croupiers' pockets, but tradition dies hard. Players now tip the waiters instead, who deduct a small handling charge and pass the money on after hours.

Then there's sex, which is also a gamble. Like coal mines, shipyards and railroads, the flesh industry has had to adapt to major changes of use and competition from other sources.

The old sellers' market has gone. People no longer expect to pay for mild titillation or casual sex encounters—not the young ones anyway, and certainly not on their home ground. With nude girls appearing in *The Times*, with explicitly sexual acts being performed nightly on the public stage (matinees on Wednesdays and Saturadys), and with copulation in living color, accompanied by a full symphony orchestra, dominating the screens of neighborhood movie theaters, London's pimps, panders and pornographers have had to repackage the product and redefine their traditional markets. The general effect of the permissive society has been to turn the industry decidedly kinky in its attempts to stay on the wrong side of conventional morality—sado-masochism is definitely "in" this year—and to concentrate its marketing effort for basic services on the out-of-town visitors' trade—tourists and businessmen with no time for preliminaries.

This escalation in the war between professionals and amateurs has left the floor shows at sex-oriented nightclubs looking curiously old-fashioned. The gorgeous strippers framed in elaborate production numbers at The Gargoyle or the Eve Club may start out with more to lose than their less fortunate sisters in Soho's sleazier strip joints, but then so do their customers, and it comes to the same in the end. Except for the textbook voyeur, there's probably as much erotic stimulation, and certainly more amusement to be had at Danny La Rue's, the nightclub home of the reigning king of the drag queens. Drag has become family entertainment in the past 10 years. There's even an annual Midsummer Dream Ball for drag queens, who are urged to book their tickets "well in advance to save disappointment, as these raves are the in-thing and heavily attended."

Soho now has as many strip joints as restaurants, and both display their menus outside. Unlike the restaurants, however, there isn't much choice between the strip joints— most of them share the same troupe of girls, who lead a very hard life. From midday to the small hours, they flit around in their orange make-up, carrying their little tote bags from one dingy basement to the next, taking it off, putting it on again, grabbing a bite here, a cup of coffee there, nodding at fellow workers on the street and brushing off with an icy glance anyone foolish enough to think their acts have much

to do with sex. It's tough on the feet and hell when it's raining.

Every joint is a club, so customers must pay a membership fee at the door as well as the price of a ticket. The
more it costs, the more you get in the way of garnish on the
meat. The girls will look less like bruised fruit, the tip-up
movie-house seats crammed in to the very edge of the tiny
stage are less likely to have been picked down nervously to
the bare foam rubber, and the acts will lead less perfunc-
torily up to the final full-frontal flourish of pubic hair. Oddly
enough, simulated intercourse, as practiced on the public
stage, has not yet reached the clubs. Kinkiness again. When
it comes to double acts, it seems that gentlemen prefer
Lesbians. And they seem to prefer them either at the Carnival club or Maxim's. (Those overpowered by a desire to
remove their own clothes in the presence of others may do
so most evenings at the Town and Country Health Salon in
Knightsbridge, although unaccompanied males may have
trouble convincing the management that their intentions are
honorable unless they hold an International Naturist Federation Passport.)

On the whole there are easier ways of seeking out uninhibited female company. Central London now bristles with
sauna and massage parlors, many of which advertise in the
Personal columns of *The Evening Standard*. But be careful—
some of them may be legitimate. The same goes for the escort agencies, which have earned a classification all to themselves in *The Standard*'s Entertainment section: "60 fabulous girls. Credit cards welcome." "An enchanting genie-girl
to bewitch you with the pleasures of London." You pay the
agency for an evening's companionship, and after that you're
on your own. It can be cheaper than combing the small
drinking clubs of Notting Hill, Bayswater and Earls Court.
But if you prefer shopping for hostesses, most taxidrivers
know the current places.

The cheapest, and most hazardous, method is to pick the
name you fancy from the vast selection of illuminated door-
bells that shine like glow-worms after dark in Soho and
Shepherd Market. Prostitution is not illegal in London, but
soliciting on the streets *is*. This means the girls must advertise. One has a red neon sign on Curzon Street offering
French lessons, and Maria has taken to displaying her phone

number, a red lamp and a photograph of herself in her window on Shepherd Street, which at least gives a prospective client some idea of what to expect. It's not exactly the Reeperbahn, however. The specialists catering to kinkier tastes, like flagellation and rubber rainwear fetishism, favor handwritten postcards in shop windows north of the park in Paddington, Bayswater and Notting Hill: "German teacher seeks new pupils. Very strict." Or "Rubber technologist offers full training course. Ring Miss Stern." Encounters on the street should always be viewed with the deepest suspicion. Any girl prepared to risk arrest is either desperate, and therefore trouble—whatever the reason—or a shill for a clip joint, which is also bad news. The preliminaries will be much the same in each case, but with one you could get rolled for your wallet by a greedy pimp, and with the other, get dumped by a bouncer on the sidewalk, full of frustration and about $25-worth of non-alcoholic fruit cup. Better by far to spend the money on a good dinner.

In general, transactions on the London fleshmarket are probably no more—or no less—satisfactory than anywhere else; whether they are ever worth the trouble is another question. Now that Londoners are so much more direct and approachable than they used to be, lone visitors ought at least to try making their way just once on traveler's charm as well as travelers' checks. They can, for instance, with perfect propriety, strike up a conversation with any of the dozens of people they are bound to come across every day, maps in hand, vainly trying to figure out how they mislaid their hotels. Conversely, a map in one's own hand and a slightly worried air is an entirely acceptable basis for accosting anybody.

Many regard the better West End pubs as happy hunting grounds in the early evening, while others—the cocktail set —generally favor hotel bars, which are in any case good jumping-off places for a night on the town, alone *or* accompanied. The Rivoli Bar at the Ritz, for instance, offers an agreeable touch of Thirties-style decadence in addition to well-mixed drinks; the Dorchester is highly thought of for similar reasons; Claridges, the Savoy or the Connaught, though not exactly pick-up parlors, are easily the most impressive for prearranged rendezvous, and even the Polo Bar at the Westbury has a devoted following, mainly because it mixes the best martinis east of the Atlantic. Slightly less obvious, and having no hotel to support, are Jules's Bar on Jermyn Street and, if you can manage on champagne, Bill Bentley's Oyster Bar on Beauchamp Place.

Later on, and failing a theater or concert, a leisurely dinner can prove an eminently agreeable way of spending an evening. In fact, there is no reason why one should not enjoy both, because London now rivals Madrid and Mexico City as a late-dining town. Reservations are usually necessary, as London also dines out a lot, but except in one or two tourist traps, tables are not hard to come by up to 9 p.m. After that, the more fashionable the restaurant, the harder it gets, until around 11 p.m. or midnight, you must either be the Aga Khan or a friend of the management to sit down at Tiberio.

London today is second only to Paris in the number, excellence and variety of its restaurants, and in value for money, way out in front. Americans are notorious, of course, for preserving their misconceptions in the teeth of the evidence, but the barely disguised condescension of some New Yorkers, for instance, when eating out in London is so ludicrously misplaced, so breathtakingly divorced from any honest comparison of restaurant standards in the two cities, as to make Washington's misjudgments in Southeast Asia seem entirely explicable.

With a few exceptions, New York specializes in obvious food coarsely cooked and indifferently served, in vulgar surroundings at extortionate cost. With a great many exceptions, London draws on fresher produce and the subtler kitchen skills of France, Italy, China and India to stage a nightly festival of the gorge at reasonable prices in some of the pleasantest settings imaginable. She's got everything: Spanish, Hungarian, Greek, German, Polish, Mexican, Indonesian, Jamaican, Japanese, Jewish, Persian, Russian, Malayan, Polynesian, Vietnamese, vegetarian—even English. She also does better hamburgers than you can get in New York—and anybody who puts ketchup on his oysters had better keep his mouth shut.

The old bad-food legend took root in the 10 years of rationing that followed World War II, and has been nourished ever since by a truly awful level of mass catering in steakhouse chains and franchise operations like Wimpy's, to which unadventurous tourists succumb in droves, presumably because they see familiar words on the menu. To judge London's culinary output by these standards is like condemning the Grenouille in New York on the strength of a White Tower burger. In fact, it's worse than that, because the Grenouille —or the Caravelle or the Côte Basque, for that matter—can't hold a candle to their London equivalents, the Mirabelle, the Caprice or the Empress. Not as restaurants, anyway. As arenas for *couture* one-upmanship, maybe.

French cooking does not, as a rule, travel any better than French chefs, but there are at least half a dozen restaurants in London up to the very best Parisian level. Two of them *are* Parisian—Le Grand Vefour and Prunier. Both are expensive, but not by New York standards (it should *be* so lucky). Memorable meals can also be had at the Etoile, Le Français, Coq d'Or and the Brompton Grill.

Italians, in contrast, transplant very readily. Franco and Mario have gone public on the strength of their vastly successful Terrazza-based empire; Alvaro has broken out of his in-group headquarters on the Kings Road to spawn a chain of *pizza e pasta* parlors, and Apicella has decorated practically every trattoria of consequence in town so that it looks like a branch of his own Meridiana. No more chianti bottles and mandolins; just white paint and rubber plants. There are hundreds to choose from, but San Lorenzo and San Martino are probably the two best family-run restaurants in London.

Except, perhaps, for the Chinese. London has been greatly blessed by the Crown Colony of Hong Kong. Gerrard Street is the heart of her new Chinatown, and Lee Ho Fook its best Cantonese restaurant (though some say the Lido). This is the kind of cooking to which most of America's Chinese restaurants aspire, usually in vain, but there is nothing in New York or San Francisco that approximates even vaguely to the rare and extravagant delights of a Peking banquet at Mr. Chow, the Gallery Rendezvous or the Dumpling Inn. Mr. Chow, who drives a Bentley convertible in a baseball cap, is a master of incongruity. At his Knightsbridge restaurant, he has teamed north China cooks synergistically with Italian waiters in the sort of ambiance which advertising agency art directors love, to produce a genuine occasion for us and a Bentley-ful of model girls for him, which seems fair. If you are unfamiliar with Peking food, let the waiters choose it. They like to watch your face as you try each dish. But insist on the duck. It takes time to prepare, but if you are in a hurry you should have gone to a Wimpy Bar anyway, and serve you right.

You may also need help in Indian restaurants. Their curries have about as much to do with what housewives make out of left-overs as Peking duck does to chop suey. The Tandoori, which specializes in Punjabi food, is very pretty and a good place either to begin one's education or to take a few post-graduate courses. The style of cooking for which the restaurant is named scores heavily with pieces of chicken marinated for 24 hours in yogurt, ginger and spices, then broiled on skewers over charcoal in a mud oven. It reduces Colonel Sanders' Southern-style product to wads of crispy-fried blotting paper.

And if you cannot decide between the Chinese way with duck and the North Indian way with chicken, the best solution is to order stuffed duck at the White Tower which is still probably the best Greek restaurant in the world and unquestionably one of the most distinguished restaurants in Europe.

Then there's the fag-type school of cookery, which has been brought into some disrepute by a plague of willowy young men mashing avocado with cream and sieved apricots before piling it back in the half-skin with a garnish of coltsfoot and chocolate sprinkles. Most of them come and go fairly quickly. But a disciplined combination of unlikely ingredients, stiffened by a backbone of classic dishes, has produced one of the best and most truly inventive restaurants of the day— Parkes. Plenty of notice and a day's fasting are essential preliminaries to a reservation. If it's booked solid all week, which is not unlikely in the high tourist season, try Carrier's or Inigo Jones instead. Both run it close competition.

The best traditional English food is still served at the Hungry Horse, and you'd better *be* hungry because the excellent soups (try the lemon fish) are served by the tureen, the vegetables arrive in droves, and the steak-and-kidney pudding won't leave much room for treacle tart. Fish is another traditional specialty, with a couple of dozen first-class seafood restaurants to choose from, including the incomparable Prunier. Scott's is pretty good too. Somewhat cheaper but still reliable are the nine Wheeler's restaurants, which boast of 18 different ways to cook sole and 11 to serve lobster. And everybody ought to try the fish and chips at Geale's, although they won't encourage you to make an evening of it.

Nor will they at The Great American Disaster, where there's always a line outside for London's best hamburgers. Nor yet at the Hard Rock Cafe, where the same hamburgers are dispensed by the same management for ravening hordes of swingers to the accompaniment of rock music loud enough to ossify the infragranular cortex. To dine there, and on the following evening at the superbly aristocratic Connaught Hotel or Wilton's, is to chart the respective polar regions of smart London society.

But if you prefer pizzas, they are served in individual sizes with a dazzling selection of fillings at the eight branches of Pizza Express, of which one is a strong contender for the title of London's handsomest cheap restaurant. Once an *art nouveau* period dairy, it stands on the corner of Coptic Street, a few yards south of the British Museum. Anybody else would have ripped out the ceramic tiled walls and buried the place in wood-grained Formica. But Pizza Express simply installed a splendid red oven as a centerpiece in the cool, lofty room, added marble-topped tables, comfortable chairs and a few potted palms, picked up the *art nouveau* feeling by painting laurel-green fronds, like stained glass, on the windows and left it at that—an exercise in restraint and good taste so rare as to deserve a knighthood at least. And on Saturday nights, you could well find yourself eating to the accompaniment of a live string quartet playing Mozart, a White Russian emigré singing balalaika songs or a Kabuki flautist and dancer.

Live entertainment with good food is a lot more expensive anywhere else and rather less fun—except at Danny La Rue's and occasionally at the Savoy Hotel, depending on who's in the floor show. Top international cabaret artists appear every night at The Talk of the Town, but there, unfortunately, you have to eat the food as well—or, at any rate, pay for it. Similar sacrifices are demanded at belly-dance restaurants. But if you're prepared to settle for a good dinner, a live combo and a bit of cheek-to-cheek, the Barracuda offers gentler treatment than its name suggests, and there's always Tiberio (late, and at a price).

On the other hand, if nothing appeals—not drama nor music, nor discos or nightclubs, casinos or strip joints, wining or dining—then it's probably past your bedtime anyway. Or else the money's running out. In which case, you might care to try one of 55 West End movie houses, an old-fashioned Turkish bath, a poetry reading, ten-pin bowling, a political demo or any of the other inexpensive happenings around town listed in *Time Out*. And when you get hungry, Tubby Isaacs will be dispensing plates of whelks and bowls of jellied eels from a corner of Aldgate, as he has for the past 40 years, and the Hungry Horse Pie Shop will be popping its customers' buttons with the cheapest blow-out on the Fulham Road.

Better yet, take what's left of the bankroll to White City Stadium for an evening's greyhound racing. More popular than horse racing, these meetings pull the biggest crowds in London, apart from soccer and Promenade concerts, and it's not hard to see why. If they want to make a night of it, people can sit behind a plate-glass window in a comfortable grandstand restaurant and have a better than average meal while they watch an all-action card of eight races in under two hours. They need not even stir from their tables to place a bet. A thoughtful management provides a team of young women to take their money to the Tote (parimutuel) and—less often—to bring it back.

But it's not just the chance of restoring the family fortune that lures so many of the faithful away from the telly. There's somehow a sharper edge of excitement than you find in horse racing when the white mechanical hare moves off, picking up speed, on its solo lap of the track. As it hurtles around the last bend, the crowd murmurs fade, then swell to a roar as the traps fly up and six numbered greyhounds catapult out, streaking off under the harsh lights in eerily silent pursuit.

The race is over in seconds. On the terraces, torn-up betting slips fall like confetti. In the grandstand, the diners return from the stakes they've lost to the steaks on their plates. And win or lose, you will know why London is going to the dogs.

$\mathcal{P}$ostscript

*I*S LONDON *really* going to the dogs?

Older Londoners think so. Of course, older Londoners have always thought so, but this time they could be right. The city they speak of belongs to the past. The special qualities they associate with London, her steadiness, her measured pace, her ample certainties, were sustained by a world which no longer exists. Like the dodo, the old London has outlived her era and cannot survive it.

But there's a lot of phoenix in her, too, and she's faced this problem before. From fixed habit, Londoners will tinker and improvise, resist the obvious and delay the inevitable, and in the end turn London into something else. Whether tourists will still want to go there when they've finished is another, and probably irrelevant, question. On present form, there should then be as much to admire in downtown Detroit. But for the moment, the city is not exactly in decline; it's more like a slow dissolve. There are hints of what will emerge when the picture clears, but the new London is mostly on paper.

Long may it remain so. If the planners have their way, Covent Garden will go, and Blackfriars and most of what's left of Bloomsbury. Piccadilly Circus, the southeast corner of Trafalgar Square, Park Lane, Hyde Park Corner, Oxford Street, Victoria, north Pimlico, the fringe of Belgravia and the entire riverfront on both banks for miles eastward of Blackfriars Bridge are all scheduled for the bulldozer. Motorways will smash through miles of London's inner suburbs. Piecemeal development will destroy the balance and character of almost every quarter so far left untouched—and for what? To adapt London to a way of life which accords a near-absolute priority to the claims of private profit and the private motor vehicle.

108

Many Londoners question that priority. There are many who feel humanity has a stronger claim, that London is above all a frame for people's lives, and that feeling at home there is more important than driving a car there. Or making a killing or working out theories there. Alarmed at the social cost of redevelopment, Londoners may yet swing the other way and settle for saner values. But they had better be quick about it, for the swing of the wreckers' ball is irreversible.

No city can stand still—least of all with a housing problem like London's. And certainly no one wants to pickle the place in schmaltz for the tourist trade—that would be foolish. But to ruin the one city left on earth where people can live in some semblance of peace with themselves and each other for the sake of what may be a passing notion of efficiency is hardly *less* stupid. If planners and architects were capable of producing by design that subtle integration of people and place that the great builders of London once achieved by art or accident, then those who value her quality might look to the future with rather more confidence.

"The intellectual man," said Boswell, "is struck with London as comprehending the whole of human life in all its variety, the contemplation of which is inexhaustible." Enough remains of the kind of London he knew for this still to be true today. But in the fading of her glory, those who would like to see for themselves had better not wait till tomorrow.

Section II
The Best of Everything

American London

UNITED STATES EMBASSY, 24 Grosvenor Square, W.1 (499-9000)

CONSUL SERVICES SECTION (Upper Grosvenor Street entrance) *Open Monday to Friday 9 am to 6 pm.*

U.S. INFORMATION SERVICE REFERENCE LIBRARY (main entrance) *Open Monday to Friday 10 am to 6 pm.*

PUBLIC LIBRARY, 3,000 books and 1,000 current U.S. periodicals.

COMMERCIAL LIBRARY (Upper Brook Street entrance).

BUSINESS ORGANIZATIONS

AMERICAN CHAMBER OF COMMERCE, 75 Brook Street, W.1 (493-0381)

LONDON CHAMBER OF COMMERCE, 69 Cannon Street, E.C.4 (248-4444)

Export advice and information:

BOARD OF TRADE, Export Services Branch, Export House, 50 Ludgate Hill, E.C.4 (248-5757)

U.S. STOCKBROKERS

MERRILL, LYNCH, PIERCE, FENNER & SMITH LTD., 25 Davies Street, W.1 (499-8172)

For list of others, contact American Embassy.

AMERICAN BANKS

AMERICAN EXPRESS CO.
  (Head Office) 6 Haymarket, S.W.1 (930-4411)
  (Commercial Banking Division) 25 Abchurch Lane, E.C.4 (623-1212)

AMERICAN NATIONAL BANK & TRUST CO. OF CHICAGO, 24 Austin Friars, E.C.2 (588-3718)

BANK OF AMERICA, 29 Davies Street, W.1 (629-7466)

BANK OF NEW YORK, 147 Leadenhall Street, E.C.3 (283-5011)

BANKERS TRUST COMPANY, 9 Queen Victoria Street, E.C.4 (248-3251)

BURSTON & TEXAS COMMERCE BANK, 41 Moorgate, E.C.2 (628-6262)

CHASE MANHATTAN, 1 Mount Street, W.1 (600-6141)

CHEMICAL BANK, 13 Davies Street, W.1 (493-2921)

CITY NATIONAL BANK OF DETROIT, 52 Cornhill, E.C.3 (626-2971)

CONTINENTAL ILLINOIS NATIONAL BANK & TRUST CO. OF CHICAGO, 58 Moorgate, E.C.2 (628-6099)

DETROIT BANK & TRUST, 1 Undershaft, St. Helen's, E.C.3 (283-4851)

FIRST CHICAGO LTD., 1 Royal Exchange Buildings, Cornhill, E.C.3 (638-8521)

FIRST NATIONAL BANK IN DALLAS, 60 Aldermanbury, E.C.2 (606-9111)

FIRST NATIONAL BANK OF BOSTON, 31 Lowndes Street, S.W.1 (235-9541)

FIRST NATIONAL BANK OF CHICAGO, 1 Royal Exchange Buildings, Cornhill, E.C.3 (283-2010)

FIRST NATIONAL CITY BANK, 17 Bruton Street, W.1 (629-6600)

FIRST NATIONAL MARYLAND & HELLER, 72 Basinghall Street, E.C.2 (606-9351)

FIRST PENNSYLVANIA BANKING & TRUST CO., 5 Trump Street, E.C.2 (606-4571)

FIRST WISCONSIN NATIONAL BANK OF MILWAUKEE, 39 New Broad Street, E.C.2 (588-7633)

FRANKLIN NATIONAL BANK, 27 Old Jewry, E.C.2 (606-1244)

HOUSTON CITIZEN'S BANK & TRUST CO., 69 King William Street, E.C.4 (626-4611)

IRVING TRUST CO., 36 Cornhill, E.C.2 (626-3210)

MANUFACTURERS HANOVER, 88 Brook Street, W.1 (491-7581)

MELLON NATIONAL BANK & TRUST, 13 Moorgate, E.C.2 (600-7291)

MORGAN GUARANTY TRUST CO., OF N.Y., 33 Lombard Street, E.C.3 (626-7890)

NATIONAL BANK OF COMMERCE OF SEATTLE, 46 Moorgate, E.C.2 (628-6671)

NATIONAL BANK OF DETROIT, 28 King Street, E.C.2 (606-4281)

REPUBLIC NATIONAL BANK OF DALLAS, 1 Moorgate, E.C.2 (606-4831)

UNITED CALIFORNIA BANK, 35 Moorgate, E.C.2 (628-9471)

WELLS FARGO BANK, 1 Broad Street Place, E.C.2 (588-3805)

WESTERN AMERICAN BANK, 18 Finsbury Circus, E.C.2 (628-3000)

CLUBS

AMERICAN CLUB, 95 Piccadilly, W.1 (499-2303)

AMERICAN WOMEN'S CLUB LTD., 1 Cadogan Gardens, S.W.3 (730-2033)
(Secretary — 730-1908)

AMERICAN SOCIETY IN LONDON, Dorchester Hotel, Park Lane, W.1 (629-8888)

AMERICAN-BRITISH ASSOCIATION (LONDON) LTD., 136 Cromwell Road, S.W.7 (373-1985)

ENGLISH-SPEAKING UNION, 37 Charles Street, W.1 (629-7400)

THE PILGRIMS, Savoy Hotel, Strand, W.C.2 (836-4343)

Archaeology

CONSTRUCTION COMPANIES hate the word. Redevelopment means digging deep holes and, in the City, deep holes mean Roman or later finds, which mean work is held up until archaeologists have sorted them out. If anything interesting is going on, the people who will know about it are:

THE GUILDHALL MUSEUM, Bassishaw Highwalk, off London Wall, E.C.2. (606-3030)
Monday to Saturday 10 am to 5 pm.

THE LONDON MUSEUM, Kensington Palace, W.8 (937-9816).
Monday to Saturday 10 am to 6 pm.
Sunday 2 pm to 6 pm.

THE CUMING MUSEUM, Walworth Road, S.E.17 (703-3324).
Monday to Friday 10 am to 5:30 pm (Thursday 7 pm).
Saturday 10 am to 5 pm.

Other useful sources of information are:

COUNCIL FOR BRITISH ARCHAEOLOGY, 8 St. Andrew's Place, Regent's Park, N.W.1 (486-1527)
Co-ordinating body for British archaeological societies. Details of current digs and type of help required from Calendar of Excavations, issued monthly from March to September, annual subscription 80p.

ROYAL ARCHAEOLOGICAL INSTITUTE, c/o London Museum, Kensington Palace, W.8
One day visits to sites of interest. Good lectures.
Informative journal published annually.

MUSEUMS AND LIBRARIES

Besides the Guildhall, London and Cuming Museums, there are also interesting archaeological collections at:

THE BRITISH MUSEUM, Great Russell Street, W.C.1 (636-1555).
Monday to Saturday 10 am to 5 pm.
Sunday 2:30 pm to 6 pm.

GUNNERSBURY PARK MUSEUM, Gunnersbury Park, W.3. (992-2247)
APRIL TO SEPTEMBER, *Monday to Friday 2 pm to 5 pm.*
Saturday, Sunday 2 pm to 6 pm.
OCTOBER TO MARCH, *daily 2 pm to 4 pm.*

The best archaeological libraries, in addition to those at the British and London Museums, are:

GUILDHALL LIBRARY, Bassishaw St., E.C.2 (606-3030)

INSTITUTE OF ARCHAEOLOGY, University of London, 31 Gordon Square, W.C.1 (387-6052)
15,000 volumes. *By appointment.*

SOCIETY OF ANTIQUARIES, Burlington House, Piccadilly, W.1 (734-0193)
130,000 volumes. *By appointment.*

INTERESTING SITES

1. Roman Baths in Lower Thames Street (opposite Billingsgate Market).
2. London Wall (a) Near St. Giles Church, Cripplegate—a corner bastion, probably medieval but the line of the Roman wall can be seen; (b) Underground Car Park—part of the west gate of the fort. Open Monday to Friday 12:30 pm to 2:30 pm.
3. Adjoining Tower Hill Tube Station—length of wall and internal turret. In adjoining gardens, reproduction of inscription from the tomb of the Procurator Classicianus found nearby.
4. Tower of London—short length of wall; bastion beneath ruined Wardrobe Tower.
5. Noble Street—outer fort wall and inner wall.
6. 8-10 Cooper's Row, E.C.3.—long stretch of wall behind Midland House.
7. All Hallows, London Wall—vestry built on a bastion of the wall.

8. St. Alphage's Churchyard, London Wall—a stretch showing the double wall at the base, and several stages of post-Roman construction.

9. St. Bride's, Fleet Street, E.C.4.—Roman pavement of mosaic in the crypt.

10. 11 Ironmonger Lane, E.C.2—Roman pavement. Ask permission to view.

11. Temple Court, Queen Victoria Street, E.C.4—Mithraic temple removed from the site of Bucklersbury House and reconstructed in the forecourt.

12. Strand Lane, W.C.2—Roman bath, restored in the 17th century.
    Monday to Saturday, 10 am to 12:30 pm.

Architecture

To EXAMINE THE FABRIC of London is to conduct a post-mortem on British architecture. Decomposition set in around the turn of the century, and by the Fifties, architects had mutated into money-box designers. Today, appearance is just a by-product of function, an abdication that might have led to interesting results if developers had been interested in any other function than maximizing rent rolls and minimizing costs. Their willing accomplices all belong to:

ROYAL INSTITUTE OF BRITISH ARCHITECTS, 66 Portland Place, W.1 (580-5533)
Extensive reference library, 60,000 volumes.
Bookshop.

Other useful sources of information for those wishing to examine the scene of the crime more closely include:

THE ARCHITECTURAL ASSOCIATION INC., 34 Bedford Square W.C.1 (636-0974)

INSTITUTE OF LANDSCAPE ARCHITECTS, 12 Carlton House Terrace, S.W.1 (839-4044)

DEPARTMENT OF THE ENVIRONMENT, Lambeth Bridge House, Albert Embankment, S.E.1. (735-7611)

GREATER LONDON COUNCIL, Department of Architecture and Civic Design, County Hall, S.E.1. (633-5000)

NATIONAL HOUSING AND TOWN PLANNING COUNCIL, 11 Green Street, W.1. (629-7107)

Preservationist groups trying to stop the rot and hang on to what's left of the greatest architectural treasury in Europe include:

THE GEORGIAN GROUP, 2 Chester Street, S.W.1. (235-3081)

SOCIETY FOR THE PROTECTION OF ANCIENT BUILDINGS, 55 Great Ormond Street, W.C.1. (405-2646)

CIVIC TRUST, 17 Carlton House Terrace, S.W.1. (930-0914)

ANCIENT MONUMENTS SOCIETY, 12 Edwardes Square, W.8. (937-1414)

THE VICTORIAN SOCIETY, 29 Exhibition Road, S.W.7. (589-7203)

BEST BUILDINGS

Anybody's list must be arbitrary, even willful. But tourists do tend to get stuck in the standard sightseeing groove of the Abbey, St. Paul's and the Tower and miss dozens of things that are just as good in their way. To encourage them to use their eyes, I suggest they try tracking these down:

OLD

1. St. Bartholomew the Great, West Smithfield, E.C.1. (circa 1140)
2. Staple Inn, High Holborn, W.C.1. (1586 onwards—much restored)
3. Banqueting House, Whitehall, S.W.1. (Inigo Jones—1619-25)
4. Greenwich Hospital, Greenwich, S.E.10. (John Webb, Wren, Vanbrugh and others 1664-1789)
5. St. Stephen Walbrook, Walbrook, E.C.4. (Sir Christopher Wren—1672-7)
6. St. Mary Abchurch, Abchurch Lane, E.C.4. (Wren—1681-6)
7. Chelsea Hospital, Chelsea Embankment, S.W.3. (Wren—1682-94)
8. New Square, Lincoln's Inn, W.C.2 (circa 1690)
9. Chandos House, Chandos Street, W.1. (Robert Adam—1769-71)
10. Woburn Walk, W.C.1. (Thomas Cubitt—1822)
11. Cumberland Terrace, N.W.1. (John Nash—1826)
12. Pelham Crescent, S.W.7. (George Basevi—1840)

Bayswater Road

Leadenhall Market

Head Shop,
Notting Hill

Portobello Road

Biba

Berwick Street

Berwick Street

Portobello Road

Portobello Road

Portobello Road

Rupert Street

Totters

Portobello Road

Portobello Road

Portobello Road

NEW

So far as I can see, there are *no* new buildings worth tracking down, except for the Post Office Tower, and that's the least difficult thing to find in all London. The Royal Institute of British Architects seems to attach some importance, however, to the following (among others):

1. Royal College of Art, South Kensington (1962-63)
   (H.T. Cadbury-Brown in association with Sir Hugh Casson and R.Y. Goodden)
2. Royal College of Physicians, Regent's Park, N.W.1 (1964)
   (Denys Lasdun & Partners)
3. Elephant House, London Zoo (1964)
   (Casson, Conder & Partners)
4. Economist buildings, St. James's, S.W.1. (1964)
   (A. & P. Smithson)
5. Office buildings for P & O Line and Commercial Union, Leadenhall Street, E.C.3 (1969)
   (Gollins, Melvin, Ward & Partners)
6. Offices, St. Katherine Dock, St. Katherine's Way, E.1. (1964)
   (Andrew Renton & Partners)
7. Offices, shops, etc., Centre Point, St. Giles's (1966)
   (R. Seifert & Partners)
8. Offices and flats, Carlton Gardens, S.W.1. (1965)
   (David Hodges, of Louis de Soissons, Peacock, Hodges, Robertson & Fraser)
9. Eros House (shops and flats), Rushey Green/Brownhill Road, Catford S.E.6 (1961)
   (Owen Luder)
10. Churchill Gardens, Pimlico, S.W.1. (1946 onwards)
    (Powell & Moya)
11. Alton Estates, Roehampton Lane, S.W.15. (1955-59)
    (GLC Architects' Department)
12. Bousfield Primary School, South Bolton Gardens, S.W.5. (1955)
    (Chamberlin, Powell & Bon)

Art

How ANY CITY could cherish the world's greatest assembly of pictures and sculptures and yet not allow it to influence everyday standards of taste and design is difficult to understand, so why try? Just marvel at the riches on show at:

1. **THE NATIONAL GALLERY,** Trafalgar Square, W.C.2 (930-7618)
   Monday to Saturday 10 am to 6 pm.
   Sunday 2 pm to 6 pm.
   (June to September, open until 9 pm. Tuesday and Thursday)

2. **THE NATIONAL PORTRAIT GALLERY,** 2 St. Martin's Place, Trafalgar Square, W.C.2 (930-8511)
   Monday to Friday 10 am to 5 pm.
   Saturday 10 am to 6 pm.
   Sunday 2 pm to 6 pm.

3. **THE TATE GALLERY,** Millbank, S.W.1 (828-1212)
   Monday to Saturday 10 am to 6 pm.
   Sunday 2 pm to 6 pm.

4. **THE WALLACE COLLECTION,** Hertford House, Manchester Square, W.1 (935-0687)
   Monday to Saturday 10 am to 5 pm.
   Sunday 2 pm to 5 pm.

5. **COURTAULD INSTITUTE PICTURE GALLERY,** Woburn Square, W.C.1. (580-1015)
   Monday to Saturday 10 am to 5 pm.
   Sunday 2 pm to 5 pm.

6. **PERCIVAL DAVID FOUNDATION OF CHINESE ART,** 53 Gordon Square, W.C.1 (387-3909)
   Monday 2 pm to 5 pm.
   Tuesday to Friday 10:30 am to 5 pm.
   Saturday 10:30 am to 1 pm.

7. **WELLINGTON MUSEUM, APSLEY HOUSE,** Hyde Park Corner, Piccadilly, W.1 (499-5676)

Monday to Saturday 10 am to 6 pm.
Sunday 2:30 pm to 6 pm.
Admission 10p.

8. **SIR JOHN SOANE'S MUSEUM,** 12/13 Lincoln's Inn Fields, W.C.2 (405-2107)
Tuesday to Saturday 10 am to 5 pm.
(Closed in August)

9. **IMPERIAL WAR MUSEUM,** Lambeth Road, S.E.1 (735-8922)
War paintings.
Monday to Saturday 10 am to 6 pm.
Sunday 2 pm to 6 pm.

These are some of the major permanent collections. At any given time, important temporary or loan exhibitions will also be open at:

1. **ROYAL ACADEMY OF ARTS,** Burlington House, Piccadilly, W.1 (734-9052)
Monday to Saturday 10 am to 6 pm.
Sunday 2 pm to 6 pm.

2. **HAYWARD GALLERY,** South Bank, S.E.1 (928-3144)
Monday to Saturday 10 am to 6 pm (8 pm Tuesday & Thursday)
Sunday 12 pm to 6 pm.

3. **INSTITUTE OF CONTEMPORY ARTS,** Nash House, The Mall, S.W.1 (930-0493)
(Hours and prices of admission vary)

4. **SERPENTINE GALLERY,** West Carriage Drive, Kensington Gardens, W.8 (402-6075)
April to September, daily 11 am to 8 pm.
October, 11 am to 6:30 pm.

5. **QUEEN'S GALLERY,** Buckingham Palace Road, S.W.1 (930-4832)
(Exhibitions from the Royal collection)
Tuesday to Saturday 11 am to 5 pm.
Sunday 2 pm to 5 pm.
Admission 15p.

6. **WHITECHAPEL ART GALLERY,** Whitechapel High Street, E.1 (247-1492)

7. **CAMDEN ARTS CENTER,** 54 Arkwright Road, N.W.3. (435-2643)

Current exhibitions at these galleries will be listed in *The Times* and *The Arts Review*. Other useful sources of information are:

1. **THE ARTS COUNCIL OF GREAT BRITAIN**, 105 Piccadilly, W.1 (629-9495)
2. **GREATER LONDON ARTS ASSSOCIATION**, 27 Southampton Street, W.C.2 (836-5225)
3. **INSTITUTE OF CONTEMPORARY ARTS**, Nash House, The Mall, S.W.1 (930-0493)
4. **THE FEDERATION OF BRITISH ARTISTS**, 17 Carlton House Terrace, S.W.1 (930-6844)
   (Its Mall Art Galleries, The Mall, S.W.1, is one of the largest given over to contemporary art in London.)
5. **ROYAL SOCIETY OF BRITISH SCULPTORS**, 8 Chesham Place, S.W.1 (235-1467)

DEALERS AND PRIVATE GALLERIES

There are far too many to cope with, even for a fanatic, but these are among the best (*The Times* or *The Arts Review* will list what's on view):

WILDENSTEIN GALLERY, 147 New Bond Street, W.1. (629-0602)

AGNEWS, 43 Old Bond Street, W.1. (629-6176)

O'HANA GALLERY, 13 Carlos Place, W.1. (499-1562)

CRANE KALMAN GALLERY, 178 Brompton Road, S.W.3. (584-7566)

KAPLAN, 6 Duke Street, St. James's, S.W.1. (930-8665)

HANOVER GALLERY, 32a St. George Street, W.1. (629-0296)

MARLBOROUGH FINE ART, 39 Old Bond Street, W.1 (629-5161)

O & P JOHNSON, Lowndes Lodge Gallery, 27 Lowndes Street, S.W.1 (235-6464)

LUMLEY CAZALET, 24 Davies Street, W.1. (499-5058)

GROSVENOR GALLERY, 48 South Molton Street, W.1 (629-0891)

REDFERN GALLERY, 20 Cork Street, W.1. (734-1732)

And keep a weather eye out for press announcements of viewing days at:

SOTHEBY'S, 34 New Bond Street, W.1. (493-8080)
CHRISTIE'S, 8 King Street, S.W.1. (839-9060)

PRINTS

MEDICI GALLERIES, 7 Grafton Street, W.1. (629-5675)
PARKER GALLERIES, 2 Albemarle Street, W.1. (499-5906)
ALECTO GALLERY, 38 Albemarle Street, W.1. (493-4226)
GANYMED PRESS, 11 Great Turnstile, W.C.1. (405-9836)

ART SERVICES

ART WORKERS GUILD, 6 Queen Square, W.C.1. (837-3474). (For any type of craftsman from painter to restorer to heraldic designer.)
CAST SERVICE, British Museum, W.C.1. (636-1555). (Cast reproductions of British Museum exhibits.)
THE GLASSHOUSE, 27 Neal Street, Covent Garden, W.C.2. (836-9785). (A studio workshop where the public can watch glass blowers and buy their work.)
THE CHELSEA POTTERY, 13 Radnor Walk, S.W.3. (352-1366). ("Open Studio" facilities, visiting potters and children welcome.)

OUTDOOR ART EXHIBITION/MARKETS

Weather permitting, the railings along Piccadilly on the north side of Green Park and along Bayswater Road on the north side of Hyde Park/Kensington Gardens are festooned on the weekends with the most appalling rubbish, but you never know—you might see something you fancy.

Books

LIKE MEN'S WEAR AND INSURANCE, books are one of the things that London does best. And not just in publishing. In London, there are more and better libraries, general and specialized, more and better bookshops, general and specialized, and more and better dealers in second-hand, out-of-print and antiquarian books than in any other city in the world.

But tourists don't normally spend much time in libraries, so two should hold them, particularly as both are prime sources of information about the rest:

BRITISH MUSEUM LIBRARY, Great Russell Street, W.C.1. (636-1555 extension 299)
Over eight million books on every subject.
Admission to the Reading Room by ticket only.
The British Museum holds one copy of every printed book published in the United Kingdom.

WESTMINSTER—CENTRAL REFERENCE LIBRARY, 2 St. Martins Street, W.C.2. (930-3274)

Browsing for books is something else. Charing Cross Road is the bookworm's paradise, and he could spend a day at least in the Farringdon Road open-air market. Here are some of the better stores and dealers:

BOOKSHOPS, General

FOYLES, 119 Charing Cross Road, W.C.2. (437-5660)
Four million volumes.

HATCHARDS, 187 Piccadilly, W.1. (734-3201)

CLAUDE GILL, 481 Oxford Street, W.1. (499-5664)

JOHN & EDWARD BUMPUS, 4 Fitzroy Square, W.1 (387-4455)

BETTER BOOKS, 94 Charing Cross Road, W.C.2. (836-6944)

W. J. BRYCE, 41 Museum Street, W.C.1. (405-5482)

TRUSLOVE & HANSON (2 branches on Sloane Street) S.W.1.

MOWBRAYS, 28 Margaret Street. W.1. (580-2812)

BOOKSHOPS, Specialized

ANTIQUARIAN

BERNARD QUARITCH, 5 Lower John Street, Golden Square, W.1 (734-0562)

E. SELIGMANN, 25 Cecil Court, W.C.2. (836-1380)

MAGGS BROTHERS, 50 Berkeley Square, W.1. (499-2007)

BERTRAM ROTA, 4-6 Savile Row, W.1. (734-3860)

PICKERING & CHATTO, 95 Wimpole Street, W.1. (636-5969)

ART/ARCHITECTURE

TIRANTI, 72 Charlotte Street, W.1. (636-8565)

ZWEMMER'S, 78 Charing Cross Road, W.C.2. (836-4710)

WEINREB & BREMAN, 92 Great Russell Street, W.C.2. (636-4895)

CHILDREN

THE CHILDREN'S BOOK CENTRE, 140 Kensington Church Street, W.8. (229-9646)

See also Harrods book department.

ECONOMICS/SCIENCE

DILLON'S UNIVERSITY BOOKSHOP, 1 Malet Street, W.C.1. (636-1577)

THE ECONOMISTS' BOOKSHOP, Clare Market, Portugal Street, W.C.2. (405-5531)

FINE BINDINGS

HATCHARDS, 187 Piccadilly, W.1. (734-3201)

E. JOSEPH, 48a Charing Cross Road, W.C.2. (836-4111)

FOREIGN

JOHN SANDOE, 10 Blacklands Terrace, Sloane Square, S.W.3. (589-9473)

HACHETTE, 4 Regent Place (off Warwick Street), W.1. (734-0798)

HISTORY

STANLEY CROWE, 5 Bloomsbury Street, W.C.1. (580-3976)

GRAHAM K. SCOTT, 2 The Broadway, Friern Barnet, N.11. (368-8568)

SIFTON PRAED, 67 St. James's Street, S.W.1. (727-0586)

LONDON

HIGH HILL BOOKSHOP, 6 Hampstead High Street, N.W.3. (435-2218)

MUSIC

TRAVIS & EMERY, 16 Cecil Court, W.C.2. (240-2129.)

OCCULT

JOHN M. WATKINS, 21 Cecil Court, Charing Cross Road, W.C.2. (836-2182)

PSYCHIC NEWS BOOKSHOP, 23 Great Queen Street, W.C.2. (405-2914)

PAPERBACKS

ASCROFT & DAW, 83 Charing Cross Road, W.C.2. (734-0950)

H. KARNAC, 58 Gloucester Road, S.W.7. (584-7908)

COLLETT'S, 52 Charing Cross Road, W.C.2. (836-2315)

POETRY

TURRET BOOKSHOP (Bernard Stone), 1b Kensington Church Walk, W.8. (937-7583)

POLITICS

COLLETT'S, 66 Charing Cross Road, W.C.2. (836-6306)

RELIGION

(Anglican) MOWBRAY'S, 28 Margaret Street, W.1. (580-2812)

(Jewish) B. HIRSCHLER, 71 Dunsmure Road, N.16. (800-6395)

THEATRICAL

ANDREW BLOCK, 20 Barter Street, W.C.1. (405-9660)

SAMUEL FRENCH (play publishers), 26 Southampton Street, W.C.2. (836-7513)

Buy British—Shopping Guide

THE GAP BETWEEN U.S. and British price levels has closed a bit in recent years, but tourists who know their way around can still count on financing at least part of their trip by taking a shopping list to London. The merchandise in the stores, shops and markets listed here either cannot be bought elsewhere or will cost you a hell of a lot more back home:

THE BIG STORES

FORTNUM & MASON, 181 Piccadilly, W.1. (734-8040)
Deservedly famous for its food and delicacies department. The Fortnum Fountain is *the* spot for snacks while shopping in the West End.

HARRODS, Brompton Road, S.W.1. (730-1234)
You name it, Harrods has it—including a zoo, bank, food halls, gigantic piano department and the trendy, unisex boutique, "Way In."

JOHN LEWIS, Oxford Street, W.1. (629-7711)
The closest thing to a go-ahead American department store. Excellent for home furnishings.

LIBERTY'S, 210 Regent Street, W.1. (734-1234)
Renowned for those Liberty prints in fabrics, clothing, scarves, ties, shirts and assorted gift possibilities.

MARKS & SPENCER, 458 Oxford Street, W.1. (486-6151)
The largest branch of this fantastic, "classless" chain. Direct from maker-to-you, the best buys in sweaters, underthings, children's clothes. Well-made, low-priced, for the whole family.

PETER JONES, Sloane Square, S.W.1. (730-3434)

Another store in the John Lewis Partnership and just as good as the parent store in Oxford Street.

SELFRIDGES, Oxford Street, W.1. (629-1234)
The Macy's of Europe.

SPECIALTY STORES

AQUASCUTUM, 100 Regent Street, W.1. (734-6090)
Classic suits, coats, tweeds and turnouts. Men and women.

AUSTIN REED, 103 Regent Street, W.1. (734-6789)
Everything teddibly British for men.

BURBERRY, 18 Haymarket, S.W.1. (930-2602)
Best for rainwear. Men and Women.

IRELAND HOUSE SHOP, 150 New Bond Street, W.1.
   (493-0428)
Ethnic, but beautiful, clothes for men, women and children.

JAEGER, 204 Regent Street, W.1. (734-4050)
They've come a long way from classic camel and cashmere.
Men and women.

LILLYWHITES, Piccadilly Circus, S.W.1 (930-3181)
Clothes and equipment with a British accent *pourle sport.*

SCOTCH HOUSE, 2 Brompton Road, S.W.1 (589-4421)
Plaids, woolens, kilts and sporrans for men, women and children.

SIMPSONS, 203 Piccadilly, W.1 (734-2002)
Daks and other well-tailored clothes for men and women.

VERY SPECIAL SHOPS

BRUSHES
   Kent, 174a Piccadilly, W.1. (493-0021)
   British brushes for hair, teeth, complexion etc.

FISHING TACKLE
Hardy, 61 Pall Mall, S.W.1. (930-7577)

GUNS
Purdey, 57 South Audley Street, W.1. (499-1801)

HANDKNITS
Women's Home Industries, 11 West Halkin Street, S.W.1 (235-3027)

MAPS
Sifton Praed, 67 St. James's Street, S.W.1 (493-0586)

MILITARY ANTIQUES
Peter Dale, 12 Royal Opera Arcade, S.W.1. (930-3695)

UMBRELLAS
Smith's, 53 New Oxford Street, W.C.1. (836-4731)

VIOLINS
W. E. Hill, 140 New Bond Street, W.1. (629-2175)

CLOTHING FOR WOMEN

COUTURE
Clive, 17 St. George Street, W.1. (499-1066)
Hardy Amies, 14 Savile Row, W.1. (734-2436)
Norman Hartnell, 26 Bruton Street, W.1. (629-0992)

BOUTIQUES
Biba, 124 Kensington High Street, W.8. (937-6287)
Beautifully designed departmentique store filled with great gear for women, men and children.
Browns, 27 South Molton Street, W.1. (499-5630)
Very expensive things of British, French and Italian origin. Men's as well as women's.
Cordoba, 134 New Bond Street, W.1. (629-5619)
Very elegant, very expensive leather fashions.
Escalade, 187a Brompton Road, S.W.3. (584-0081)
High-priced supermarket filled with expensive clothes, accessories and an American-styled Hamburgeria.

Foale & Tuffin, 1 Marlborough Court, W.1. (437-0087)
Two of Britain's best young designers in their own shop.

Lucienne Phillips, 69 Knightsbridge, S.W.1. (520-7931)
A good selection of expensive, designer clothes.

Marrian-McDonnell, 45 South Molton Street, W.1. (499-3363)
Moderately priced clothes by the two young men who own
this shop.

Boston 151, 151 Fulham Road, S.W.3. (589-7481)
Up-market clothes for up-market people at up-market prices.

Wallis Shops, 490 Oxford Street, W.1. (629-2171)
A chain with smart, mass-priced clothing and twice-a-year
"pick of Paris" copies.

SHOES

Anello & Davide, 96 Charing Cross Road, W.C.2. (836-5019)
A dancers' shoe shop with lots of good-looking civvies as
well.

Chelsea Cobbler, 165 Draycott Avenue, S.W.3. (584-9794)
Very in for weird shoes. Will cobble to order as well.

Elliots, 76 New Bond Street, W.1. (629-3644)
The only shoe shop in London carrying narrow widths.
Marvelous boots.

Russell & Bromley, 24 New Bond Street, W.1. (629-6903)
Excellent selection of shoes and boots.

HATS

Herbert Johnson, 38 New Bond Street, W.1. (629-7177)

Malyard, 3 Kingly Street, W.1. (437-1848)

CLOTHING FOR MEN

TAILORS

Anderson & Sheppard, 30 Savile Row, W.1. (734-1420)

Douglas Hayward, 95 Mount Street, W.1. (499-5574)

Huntsman & Sons, 11 Savile Row, W.1. (734-7441)

Kilgour French & Stanbury, 33a Dover Street, W.1. (629-
4283)

HABERDASHERS

Beale & Inman, 131 New Bond Street, W.1. (629-4723)

Blades, 8 Burlington Gardens, W.1. (734-8911)

Conways, 91 Jermyn Street, S.W.1. (930-9174)

Hawes & Curtis, 2 Burlington Gardens, W.1. (493-3803)

John Michael, 18 Savile Row, W.1. (734-0831)

Mister Fish, 17 Clifford Street, W.1. (734-9311)

Turnbull & Asser, 71 Jermyn Street, S.W.1. (930-0502)

BOUTIQUES

TOO NUMEROUS TO MENTION so walk along the King's Road, Kensington Church Street, and, yes, even Carnaby Street for shops like Just Men, Village Gate and John Stephens.

SHOES

Alan McAfee, 38 Dover Street, W.1. (493-1771)

Codner, Coombs & Dobbie, 21 Jermyn Street, W.1. (734-1383)

Church's, 58 Burlington Arcade, W.1. (493-8307)

C H E M I S T S

Maitlands, 175 Piccadilly, W.1. (493-1975)
Specializes in loofahs and sponges.

Nelson & Co., 75 Duke Street, W.1. (629-3118)
London's only homeopathic medicine shop.

Savory & Moore, 143 New Bond Street, W.1. (629-4471)
London's handsomest chemist shop.

C H I L D R E N

CLOTHES

Mothercare, 461 Oxford Street, W.1. (629-6621)
The best of cheap clothes for very young kids.

Rowe, 120 New Bond Street, W.1. (734-9711)
The other side of the class coin for your little Lord or Lady Fauntleroy.

TOYS

Beatties, 112 High Holborn, W.C.1. (405-6285)
Model railway equipment, new and old. Many of the children shopping here are well over 40.

Hamley's, 200 Regent Street, W.1. (734-3161)
More toys, games, books and gadgets than seems possible or even sensible.

EDIBLES

CHOCOLATES

Charbonnel et Walker, 31 Old Bond Street, W.1. (629-5149)
House of Floris, 39 Brewer Street, W.1. (437-5155)
Prestats, 24 South Molton Street, W.1. (629-4838)

CHEESE

Paxton & Whitfield, 93 Jermyn Street, S.W.1. (930-3380)

COFFEE & TEA

Moore Bros., 175 Brompton Road, S.W.3. (589-1833)

Higgins, 42 South Molton Street, W.1. (629-3913)

GROCERIES

Jacksons, 171 Piccadilly, W.1. (493-1033)
By appointment to H.M. the Queen. Also carries nice kitchen-ware.

Leons, 6 Marylebone High Street, W.1. (486-1134)
Hershey's Chocolate Kisses, Ivory Soap and other American items for the homesick heart, soul and stomach.

ANTIQUES

LONDON IS ANTIQUESVILLE STILL. Best bet is to roam the neighborhoods and markets that specialize. Some of the best are Bond Street, Fulham Road, Islington, Hampstead, Kensington Church Street, King's Road, Pimlico Road, Portobello Road and Westbourne Grove.

JEWELRY

Hooper Bolton, 8a Sloane Street, S.W.1. (235-4975)

Modern, original British jewelry.

Cameo Corner, 26 Museum Street, W.C.1. (636-0401)
Rare and old pieces from inexpensive to very.

Electrum Gallery, 21 South Molton Street, W.1. (629-6325)
Modern jewelry by leading designers from Britain and abroad.

Greens, 117 Kensington Church Street, W.8. (229-9618)
Lovely odd bits of antique jewelry with many rings.

Andrew Grima, 80 Jermyn Street, S.W.1. (839-2156)
More modernity.

S. J. Phillips, 139 New Bond Street, W.1. (629-6261)
One of the best of those fantastic London, antique jewel shops. One-of-a-kind pieces at one-of-a-kind prices.

Or just go wandering down Burlington Arcade, through the antique markets or around Hatton Garden—the wholesale jewelry area.

FRAGRANCES

Culpepper, 21 Bruton Street, W.1. (629-4559)
All things herbal from cosmetics to edibles.

Floris, 89 Jermyn Street, S.W.1. (930-2885)
Home of those famous Floris fragrances.

Taylor of London, 166 Sloane Street, S.W.1. (235-4653)
Makers of lovely English scents.

TOBACCO

Dunhill, 30 Duke Street, S.W.1. (493-9161)
Pipes, cigars, tobaccos.

James J. Fox, 2 Burlington Gardens, W.1. (493-9009)
Cigar specialists.

Fribourg & Treyer, 34 Haymarket, S.W.1. (930-1305)
A tobacco and snuff shop worth seeing as well as shopping.

Smiths Snuff Shop, 74 Charing Cross Road, W.C.2. (836-7422)
Entrancing even if you don't sniff the stuff.

HOUSE AND HOME

CHINA
Chinacraft, 499 Oxford Street, W.1. (499-9881)
Rosenthals, 137 Regent Street, W.1. (734-3076)
Thomas Goode, 19 South Audley Street, W.1. (499-2823)

LINENS
The White House, 51 New Bond Street, W.1. (629-3521)
Robinson & Cleaver, 158 Regent Street, W.1. (734-7262)

SILVER
Aspreys, 165 New Bond Street, W.1. (493-6767)
Garrard, 112 Regent Street, W.1. (734-7020)
Shrubsole, 43 Museum Street, W.C.1. (405-2712)

WALLPAPER
Coles, 18 Mortimer Street, W.1. (580-1066)

MARKETS

INDOOR
Antiquarius, 135 Kings Road, S.W.3
Good antiques, handsomely presented.
Closed Monday.

Antique Hypermarket, 26 Kensington High Street, W.8.
Three floors of hyperpriced antiques.
Open daily.

Antiques Supermarket, St. Christopher's Place, Barrett
   Street, W.1.
Pricey. Jewelry, furniture and bits.
Open daily.

Chelsea Antique Market, 253 Kings Road, S.W.3.
From furniture to fashion.
Open daily.

Kensington Market, Kensington High Street, W.8.
Lots of old clothes and young kids.
Open daily.

Mayfair Antique Market, Shepherd Market, W.1.

Small market, small objets d'art, large prices.
Open daily.

OUTDOOR

Bermondsey (Caledonian Market), Tower Bridge Road to Bermondsey Street, S.E.1.
The antique dealer's antique market. Come early.
Open 6 am to 1 pm Fridays.

Berwick Street, W.1. (off Piccadilly end of Shaftesbury Avenue)
Fruits, vegetables and local color.
Open daily.

Church Street, N.W.8. (off Lisson Grove)
Junk.
Open daily.

Club Road, E.1. (Sclater Street off Bethnal Green Road)
Animal and bird market.
Open 8:30 am to 1 pm Sundays.

Camden Passage, N.1.
Antiques, bits and bobs. Getting expensive.
Open Wednesdays and Saturdays.

Leather Lane, E.C.1.
General goods.
Open daily.

Petticoat Lane, E.1. (Middlesex Street)
Food, clothes, household wares. Famous Sunday outing.
Open 8 am to 2 pm Sundays.

Portobello Road, W.10.
The most famous market. Antiques, bric-a-brac, jewelry, clothes, junk.
Open Saturdays.

Shepherd Market, W.1.
A series of shops and stalls, in-and-out-of-doors.
Open daily.

The Cut, S.E.1. (off Waterloo Road)
Household, junk.
Open 9 am to 4 pm daily.

Calendar—London Events

SOMETHING IMPROBABLE is always going on in London. Tourists with an eye for the bizarre and romantic could time their visits, for instance, to coincide with swan-upping or the Coster-mongers' Harvest Festival. Others, of a more practical bent, might like to celebrate Karl Marx's birthday in Highgate Cemetery or take in the Business Efficiency Exhibition. Whatever their interests, this calendar should help them decide. Once there, fuller information can be had from the sources listed under Tourist Services.

DAILY CEREMONIES

Changing of the Guard, Horse Guards Parade, Whitehall, S.W.1
Takes place daily at 11 am (10 am Sunday).

The Changing of the Queen's Guard at Buckingham Palace, S.W.1.
Every day at 11:30 am with music.
When the Royal Standard is not flying the ceremony is held in Friary Court, St. James's Palace, at 10:30 am.

The Ceremony of the Keys, Tower of London, E.C.3.
This 700-year-old ceremony can be watched on written application to the Resident Governor, HM Tower of London, E.C.3.

ANNUAL EVENTS

JANUARY

New Year's Day: Cloker Bequest Service at St. Magnus the Martyr, Upper Thames Street, E.C.4. Annual service and reading of the will of Mr. Henry Cloker, dated 1573, attended by the Masters, Wardens and Liverymen of the Coopers' Company. The will established a charity administered by the Company.

January 6: Royal Epiphany Service. Sovereign attends either in person or by proxy at the Chapel Royal, St. James's Palace, Marlborough Road, S.W.1. Two Gentlemen Ushers offer gold, frankincense and myrrh on behalf of the Queen in a ceremony dating back to at least 1730.

January 30: Service for the Royal Martyr. The ceremony takes place at the foot of the equestrian statue of Charles I in Trafalgar Square at the head of Whitehall. Wreaths are also laid outside the Banqueting House.

Early January: Old Bailey in Session. The Lord Mayor goes in full state from the Mansion House to the Central Criminal Court, Old Bailey, E.C.4, attended by Sheriffs, the Sword-bearer, Common Crier and City Marshall.

Early January: International Boat Show at Earls Court, S.W.5.

During January: Before the first meeting of the City of London's newly elected Court of Common Council, the Lord Mayor attends a short service of dedication at the church of St. Lawrence Jewry, Gresham Street, E.C.2, accompanied by the Sheriffs, Aldermen, High Officers and members of the Court of Common Council. The company goes to the church in procession from Guildhall.

During January: The Lord Mayor is presented with a boar's head by the Butchers' Company, and a lamb by the Tenants' Association at Smithfield Market.

During January: Schoolboy's Own Exhibition at Olympia, W.14.

During January: National Stamp Exhibition at Central Hall, Westminster.

FEBRUARY

February 3: Blessing of Throats. On St. Blaise's Day, there is a ceremony at the Church of St. Ethelreda, Ely Place, Holborn, at which those suffering from throat afflictions have their throats blessed by a priest holding two candles tied in the form of a cross.

February 6: Artillery salute at the Tower to mark the anniversary of the Queen's accession.

February 20: Sir John Cass Founder's Day Service. When making his will in 1718, in which he provided for many charities, Sir John Cass was seized with a hemorrhage, staining his quill pen with blood. At the annual memorial service held for him in the church of St. Botolph, Aldgate, students of the Sir John Cass College wear red feather quills in their hats and lapels.

Shrove Tuesday: Pancake races along the Embankment. Soho waiters in pancake-tossing competition.

Ash Wednesday: Court and Livery of the Stationers' Company attend service in the crypt of St. Paul's Cathedral.

Early February: Cruft's Dog Show, Olympia.

MARCH

March 5: Karl Marx's birthday celebrated at Highgate Cemetery, N.6.

March 21: The Druids celebrate the spring equinox at midday on Tower Hill, near the site of the ancient burial ground, Bryn Gwyn.

During March: Daily Mail Ideal Home Exhibition, Olympia.

During March: Spring Antiques Fair, Chelsea Town Tall, King's Road, S.W.3 (352-8101).

End of March: Oranges & Lemons Service. Special service at the Church of St. Clement Danes, Strand, W.C.2. (242-8282), after which oranges and lemons are distributed to children.

End of March: John Stow Commemoration Service. St. Andrew Undershaft, Leadenhall Street, E.C.3. On a date near the anniversary of the death of Elizabethan writer, John Stow, the Lord Mayor and Sheriffs attend a service at which the Lord Mayor places a new quill in the hand of Stow's statue in the presence of children from various London schools competing in the annual John Stow Essay Contest. The school with the winning pupil is presented with the old quill by the Lord Mayor.

MARCH / APRIL

Oxford vs. Cambridge Boat Race on the River Thames from Putney to Mortlake.

Maundy Thursday: Royal Maundy Money is distributed by a member of the Royal family on even-numbered years at Westminster Abbey, S.W.1 (222-1051). The recipients are chosen from the London poor and the specially struck coins, handed out in small purses, are promptly sold to dealers.

Good Friday: Widow's Son Inn, Devons Road, Bromley-by-Bow, E.3. The first sailor to enter the pub adds a hot-cross bun to the 140-year-old collection hanging from the ceiling. This is followed by a general distribution of hot-cross buns to the patrons.

Butterworth Charity. After a service at St. Bartholomew the Great, Smithfield, E.C.1, at 11 am, coins and hot-cross buns are distributed in the churchyard among poor widows of the parish.

Easter Sunday: Parade, Battersea Park, S.W.11. Colorful carnival procession.

London Horse Harness Parade, Regent's Park, H.W.1.

Easter Monday: Bank Holiday Fair, Hampstead Heath.

APRIL

April 9: Budget Day. The Chancellor of the Exchequer leaves No. 11 Downing Street on his way to the House of Commons carrying the traditional red dispatch box for the crowds to see.

April 23: St. George's Day service in St. Paul's Cathedral for the Knights and Companions of the Most Distinguished Order of St. Michael and St. George in full ceremonial dress. The nave and south transept are open to the public.

Second Wednesday after Easter: Spital Sermon at St. Lawrence Jewry. The Lord Mayor walks in procession from Guildhall.

Around April 26: William Shakespeare Service at Southwark Cathedral, S.E.1.

Last Sunday: A procession from Newgate Prison to the site of Tyburn gallows at Marble Arch. This pilgrimage by Roman Catholic clergy and laity follows the route taken by the victims of the religious persecutions of the 16th and 17th centuries.

Mid-month: Royal Horticultural Society Spring Flower Show, Royal Horticultural Society Hall, Vincent Square, S.W.1. (834-4333).

The Greyhound Grand National, White City, Wood Lane, W.12. (743-7220).

MAY

May 1: Labor Party and left-wing political rally and procession to Hyde Park.

May 21: Lilies and Roses Ceremony at the Tower of London to commemorate the murder of Henry VI in 1471. Representatives of Eton and King's College, Cambridge, walk in procession to Wakefield Tower to place the traditional lilies and red roses on the spot where the murder occurred.

May 29: Oak-Apple Day at Royal Hospital, Chelsea, S.W.3. Chelsea pensioners honor their founder, Charles II. His statue in the main court is decorated with oak branches, and sprigs of oak are worn, in memory of Boscobel oak in which the King hid after the Battle of Worcester in 1651. After a march-past and inspection, the pensioners in their long red coats and tricorn hats sit down to their Founder's Day plum pudding and pint of beer.

First Saturday in the month: Crowning of the London May Queen on Hayes Common, Bromley. Procession by some 2,000 children.

First Sunday: Vintage commercial vehicles leave from the British Transport Museum, Clapham High Street, S.W.4. for their annual run to Brighton.

Second Saturday: Soccer Cup Final, Empire Stadium, Wembley, Middlesex.

Third Sunday: Stock Exchange annual London to Brighton walk, starting at Westminster Bridge.

Mid-May: Summer Art Exhibition, Royal Academy, Burlington House, Piccadilly, W.1. (734-7981).

Mid-May: Richmond Royal Horse Show, Richmond, Surrey.

Last Monday: Bank Holiday. Sheepdog Trials, Hyde Park, W.2. Bank Holiday Fair, Hampstead Heath.

Late May: Chelsea Flower Show, Royal Hospital, South Grounds, S.W.3. (730-7036).

The greatest display of flowers in the world and the high point of the Royal Horticultural Society's year.

MAY/JUNE

Derby Day, Epsom Downs, Surrey. The Londoner's big, boozy, booming day at the races.

JUNE

June 3 and 7: Beating Retreat on Horse Guards Parade, S.W.1.

June 10: Prince Philip's birthday, artillery salute in Hyde Park.

Following Saturday: Queen's official birthday marked by Trooping the Color on Horse Guards Parade. (Full rehearsal two days before.) This is one of Britain's most spectacular displays of military pageantry. Seats, almost unobtainable, are by ticket only.

June 24: Election of Sheriffs. Since 1475, two Sheriffs and other officers have been elected annually by the Liverymen of each of the City Livery Companies at a ceremony called Common Council. This takes place in the Great Hall of Guildhall, and posies are carried to ward off the plague. (Tickets from Keeper of Guildhall, Guildhall, Gresham Street, E.C.2.)

June 24: Procession of Knights of St. John at St. John's Gate, Clerkenwell, E.C.1.

First weekend: Open Air Art exhibition opens at Heath Street, N.W.3.

Mid-June: Royal Ascot Week. Horse racing at Ascot, Berkshire. Pinnacle of the social season.

Mid-June: Cricket Test Match, Lord's, St. John's Wood Road, N.W.8. (289-1615).

Mid-June: Antique Dealers Fair, Grosvenor House, Park Lane, W.1. (499-6363).

Late June: Knollys Rose Presentation. This ceremony commemorates the quit-rent, imposed in 1381, by the then Lord Mayor on the wife of Sir Robert Knollys, who built a bridge from her house in Seething Lane to a property across the road. The members of the Ward of Tower and the parishioners of All Hallows, Barking-by-the-Tower, present a single red rose to the Lord Mayor at Mansion House. The Lady Mayoress receives a bouquet of roses.

JUNE/JULY

All-England Lawn Tennis Championships, Church Road, Wimbledon, S.W.19 (946-2244).

Henley Royal Regatta, Henley-on-Thames, Oxfordshire.

JULY

July 10: The "crowning" of the Master and Wardens of the Grocers' Company, preceded by a service in St. Margaret Lothbury, Lothbury, E.C.2.

July 25: On the feast day of St. Christopher, cars line up outside the church of St. Michael Paternoster Royal, College Hill, E.C.4. so that their occupants may receive a blessing and prayers for protection from the hazards of the road.

Mid-July: Swan Upping. In traditional costume, the Swan Masters and their assistants boat up-river from London Bridge to Henley taking a census of swans. Cygnets belonging to two City Companies are given nicks on their beaks— one for the Dyers and two for the Vintners. The Queen's birds are left unmarked but recorded.

Mid-July: Royal International Horse Show, White City, W.12 (743-7220).

Mid-July: AAA Championships (Athletics) at Crystal Palace, S.E.19.

Mid-July: Royal Tournament, Earls Court (385-1234).

Mid-July: National Rose Society Annual Show. Alexandra Palace, N.10 (883-9711).

Late July: Doggets Coat and Badge Race, sometimes called the "Waterman's Derby." Oldest organized race in English history—by rowboat on the Thames from London Bridge to Chelsea.

Late July: Sir Henry Wood Promenade Concerts begin at the Royal Albert Hall, Kensington Gore, S.W.7. (589-8212).

During July: Road Sweeping by the Vintners Company. Following the installation of the new Master of the Vintners Company, a procession goes from the Vintners Hall to St. James's Garlickhythe, Garlick Hill, E.C.4. (236-1719), headed by Wine Porters in white smocks. They sweep a passage clean with besom brooms for members of the Court, who carry bouquets of sweet herbs.

AUGUST

Mid-August: Cricket, Test Match at the Oval, S.E.11 (735-2424).

Mid-August: Royal Horticultural Society Summer Flower Show, Royal Horticultural Society Halls, Vincent Square, S.W.1.

Last Monday: Public Holiday. Greater London Horse Show, Clapham Common, S.W.4.

Bank Holiday Fair, Hampstead Heath.

During August: Cart Marking, Guildhall Yard, E.C.2. City of London Street traders annual gathering for renewal of licenses. Carts are marked with the City arms on the shafts and numbered on a brass plate.

SEPTEMBER

September 15: Battle of Britain Week. R.A.F. fly-past over Westminster between 11 am and 12 pm. (Thanksgiving service at Westminster Abbey, S.W.1. on the following Sunday.)

September 21: Christ's Hospital Boys' March. On St. Matthew's Day, a service is held at St. Sepulchre's Church, Holborn Viaduct, E.C.1, attended by the Lord Mayor, Sheriffs and Aldermen, the Bluecoat Boys from the Horsham School and 25 girls from the Hertford School wearing their traditional Tudor uniforms—dark-blue gown, white linen bands and yellow stockings. A procession of 300 pupils, headed by the school band, afterwards proceeds to Mansion House.

September 23: The Druids celebrate the Autumn Equinox at Primrose Hill, N.W.1.

September 28: Admission of Sheriffs. The Sheriffs Elect, attended by the Liverymen of their Companies, come to Guildhall in a procession consisting of senior members of the Corporation, the Aldermen, accompanied by their Ward beadles in livery and carrying the Ward Maces, and the Lord Mayor, who is preceded by his three Household Officers— the Sword Bearer, the Common Crier and Serjeant-at-Arms (who carries the Mace) and the City Marshall.

September 29: Election of Lord Mayor. This ceremony, called Common Hall, takes place in the Guildhall, preceded by a procession from St. Lawrence Jewry, Gresham Street, E.C.2.

Mid-September: Last night at the Proms, Royal Albert Hall. (Season ticket holders, ticket-ballot winners and standees only.)

Late September: Autumn Antiques Fair, Chelsea Old Town Hall, Kings Road, S.W.3 (352-8101).

During September: Royal Horticultural Society Great Autumn

Show. Royal Horticultural Society Halls, Vincent Square, S.W.1 (834-4333).

OCTOBER

October 1: Law Courts open. Service at Westminster Abbey, S.W.1 (222-1051), followed by a procession through the main hall of the Royal Courts of Justice, Strand, W.C.2.

October 3: The Lord Chancellor, on behalf of the Sovereign, receives the Lord Mayor Elect at the House of Lords, and conveys to him Her Majesty's approval of his election. Procession from House of Lords to Westminster Abbey for Service.

First Sunday: Costermongers' Harvest Festival at St. Martin-in-the-Fields, Trafalgar Square, W.C.2 (930-1862). Service attended by Pearly Kings and Queens.

First Sunday: Harvest of the Sea Thanksgiving at St. Mary-at-Hill, Lovat Lane, E.C.3 (624-4184). Church is decorated by the fish merchants of Billingsgate Market.

October 13: Feast of King Edward the Confessor. Service at Westminster Abbey, which he founded in the year 1050.

October 16: Lion Service at St. Katherine Creechurch, Leadenhall Street, E.C.3. to commemorate Sir John Gayer's miraculous deliverance from a lion whilst traveling with a caravan of merchants in Arabia. Buried in the church in 1694, he left money to provide for a sermon to be preached every year on the anniversary of his deliverance.

October 21: Trafalgar Day Celebrations. In commemoration of the Battle of Trafalgar, 1805, a naval parade proceeds from the Mall to Trafalgar Square, where there is a short service and wreaths are placed at the foot of Nelson's Column.

During October: Service in St. Margaret Pattens, Eastcheap, E.C.3. to mark the election of the Prime Warden of the Worshipful Company of Basketmakers.

Late October: Quit Rents Ceremony. Law Courts, Strand, W.C.2. The Queen's Remembrancer receives from the City Solicitor: first, a bill-hook and a hatchet, as quit-rent for a piece of land called the Moors, in Shropshire; and second, six horseshoes and 61 nails, which have been tendered annually since 1234 as quit-rents to the Crown for the site of a forge outside St. Clement Danes church.

During October: Horse of the Year Show, Wembley Stadium, Wembley, Middlesex (902-1234).

International Motor Show, Earls Court.

Business Efficiency Exhibition, Olympia.

International Dairy Show, Olympia.

NOVEMBER

Early November: State Opening of Parliament. The Queen, with an escort of Household Cavalry, drives in the Irish State Coach from Buckingham Palace to Westminster via The Mall and Whitehall.

November 5: Guy Fawkes' Day. Much burning of bonfires and exploding of fireworks in honor of an unsuccessful attempt to blow up Parliament in 1605.

First Sunday: R.A.C. Veteran Car Run from London (*Hyde Park Corner at 8 am*) to Brighton.

November 11 (or nearest Sunday): Remembrance Day Service at the Cenotaph, Whitehall, S.W.1. Salute of guns.

Second Friday: Guildhall. Admission ceremony of the Lord Mayor. Known as the "silent change," for apart from a Declaration of Office to the City, no words are spoken. The outgoing Lord Mayor ceremoniously hands the City Insignia to his successor. The bells of the City ring out, trumpeters sound a fanfare, and the two principals travel back to the Mansion House together. (Tickets from Keeper of Guildhall, Guildhall, Gresham Street, E.C.2.)

Second Saturday: Lord Mayor's Procession and Show. The newly elected Lord Mayor is driven in state in a 200-year-old gilded coach from the Guildhall to the Law Courts to take the oath before the Lord Chief Justice and the Judges of the Queen's Bench. The Company of Pikemen and Musketeers forms his bodyguard, and a procession is made up of liveried footmen, coachmen and decorated floats. *The procession leaves the Guildhall at about 11:30 am.*

November 22: St. Cecilia's Festival. Service at church of St. Sepulchre, Holborn Viaduct, attended by Lord Mayor and Sheriffs. The observances include an evening concert of English music at the Albert Hall.

During November: National Chrysanthemum Society's Show, Royal Horticultural Society Halls, Vincent Square, S.W.1.

DECEMBER

December 4-8: Royal Smithfield Show, Earls Court (agricultural livestock).

December 16 onwards: Carol singing, Trafalgar Square, *most evenings.*

December 25: Christmas Day services. *Almost everything closed down.*

December 26: Boxing Day. Public holiday. Theaters reopen.

Mid-December: Richmond Championship Dog Show, Olympia.

Late December: The Australian High Commissioner presents a grand Christmas Pudding to the Lord Mayor, who donates it to charity. A children's party is held at Mansion House.

During December: Christmas Cheeses. The Chelsea Pensioners each receive a tankard of beer and a piece of cheese. Instructions to supply the "cheese from Gloucester at 3d. per lb." were originally laid down in 1691.

December 31: Piccadilly, W.1. Trafalgar Square, W.C.2. "Auld Lang Syne," drunken revelry and fountain-bathing by massed crowds.

Gathering of Scouts outside St. Paul's Cathedral, *10 pm to midnight.*

Films

IF YOU ENJOY GOING TO THE MOVIES but don't fancy any of the 250-odd films listed as current attractions in *Time Out*, don't despair—there are always the cinema clubs to fall back on.

These are some of the better ones (but check first—most of them require you to be a member for an hour or so before you can get in):

NATIONAL FILM THEATRE, South Bank, Waterloo, S.E.1 (928-3232).

STARLIGHT CLUB, Mayfair Hotel, Berkeley Street, W.1 (629-7777).

THE NEW CINEMA CLUB, 122 Wardour Street, W.1 (734-5888).

THE ELECTRC CINEMA CLUB, 191 Portobello Road, W.11 (727-4992).

THE OTHER CINEMA, 12-13 Little Newport Street, W.C.2 (734-5808).

Complete listings and other information may be had from the British Federation of Film Societies, 81 Dean Street, W.1 (437-4355).

Help!

These Numbers Are Useful in Emergencies

POLICE, FIRE, AMBULANCE

DIAL 999, tell the operator which service you require.

DISTRESS ORGANIZATIONS

ALCOHOLICS ANONYMOUS—*24 hour service* (352-9669).

GAMBLERS ANONYMOUS—*24 hour service* (222-4252).

SUICIDES ANONYMOUS (Samaritans)—*24 hour service* (626-9000, 626-2277).

OPENLINE (personal crises)—*24 hour service* (night 930-1732, day 930-4137).

RELEASE (police, drug problems, etc.)—*24 hour service* (603-8654).

BIT (general advice, including crash pads)—*24 hour service* (229-8219).

RAC (automobile problems)—*24 hour service* (930-4343).

AA (automobile problems)—*24 hour service* (954-7373).

UNITED STATES EMBASSY (and why not?)—(499-9000).

ALL-NIGHT PHARMACIES

BOOTS, Piccadilly Circus, W.1 (930-4761).

JOHN BELL & CROYDEN, 50 Wigmore Street, W.1 (935-5555).

ALL-NIGHT POST OFFICE

KING WILLIAM IV STREET, Trafalgar Square, W.C.2 (930-9580).

EMERGENCY MEDICAL TREATMENT

Don't try to find a doctor. Dial 999 and you will be advised of your nearest hospital. Central hospitals operating 24 hours a day include:

ST. GEORGE'S HOSPITAL, Hyde Park Corner, S.W.1 (235-4343).
CHARING CROSS HOSPITAL, Agar Street, Strand, W.C.2 (836-7788).
MIDDLESEX HOSPITAL, Mortimer Street, W.1 (636-8333).
UNIVERSITY COLLEGE HOSPITAL, Gower Street, W.C.1 (387-9300).

EMERGENCY DENTAL TREATMENT

(NIGHT) St. George's Hospital, Tooting, S.W.17 (672-1255).
(DAY) Royal Dental Hospital of London, 32 Leicester Square, W.C.2 (930-8831).

EMERGENCY ACCOMMODATION

HOTAC—*weekdays 10 am to 10 pm (May-October)*
10 am to 6 pm (November-April)
(935-2555)

Hotels

IF YOU CAN POSSIBLY AVOID IT, don't go to London without a reservation. In spite of all the new hotels, there is still a high-season shortage of beds, particularly in the middle price range.

There are no bargains either. If you have to ask what the room rates are, don't bother with these:

SIX OF THE BEST DE LUXE HOTELS

BERKELEY, Wilton Place, S.W.1 (235-6000).
CLARIDGES, Brook Street, W.1 (629-8860).
CONNAUGHT, 36 Carlos Place, W.1 (499-7070).
DORCHESTER, Park Lane, W.1 (629-8888).
RITZ, Piccadilly, W.1 (493-8181).
SAVOY, Strand, W.C.2 (836-1533).

You won't save much if you settle for one of these:

SIX ACCEPTABLE SUBSTITUTES

BROWNS, Dover Street, W.1 (493-6020).
HYDE PARK, 66 Knightsbridge, S.W.1 (235-2000).
INN ON THE PARK, Hamilton Close, W.1 (499-0888).
SONESTA TOWER, Cadogan Place, S.W.1 (235-5411).
STAFFORD, St. James's Place, S.W.1 (493-0111).
WESTBURY, New Bond Street, W.1 (629-7755).

But for a sensible blend of price, comfort and convenience, you could do a lot worse than try these:

CADOGAN, 75 Sloane Street, S.W.1 (235-7141).
DURRANTS, 26 George Street, W.1 (935-8131)
INTERNATIONAL, Lancaster Gate, W.2 (262-3121).
LONDONER, Welbeck Street, W.1 (935-4442).
PORTOBELLO HOTEL, 22 Stanley Gardens, W.11 (727-2777).
WHITES, 90 Lancaster Gate, W.2 (262-2711).

If they're all full, or too expensive, go into a huddle with

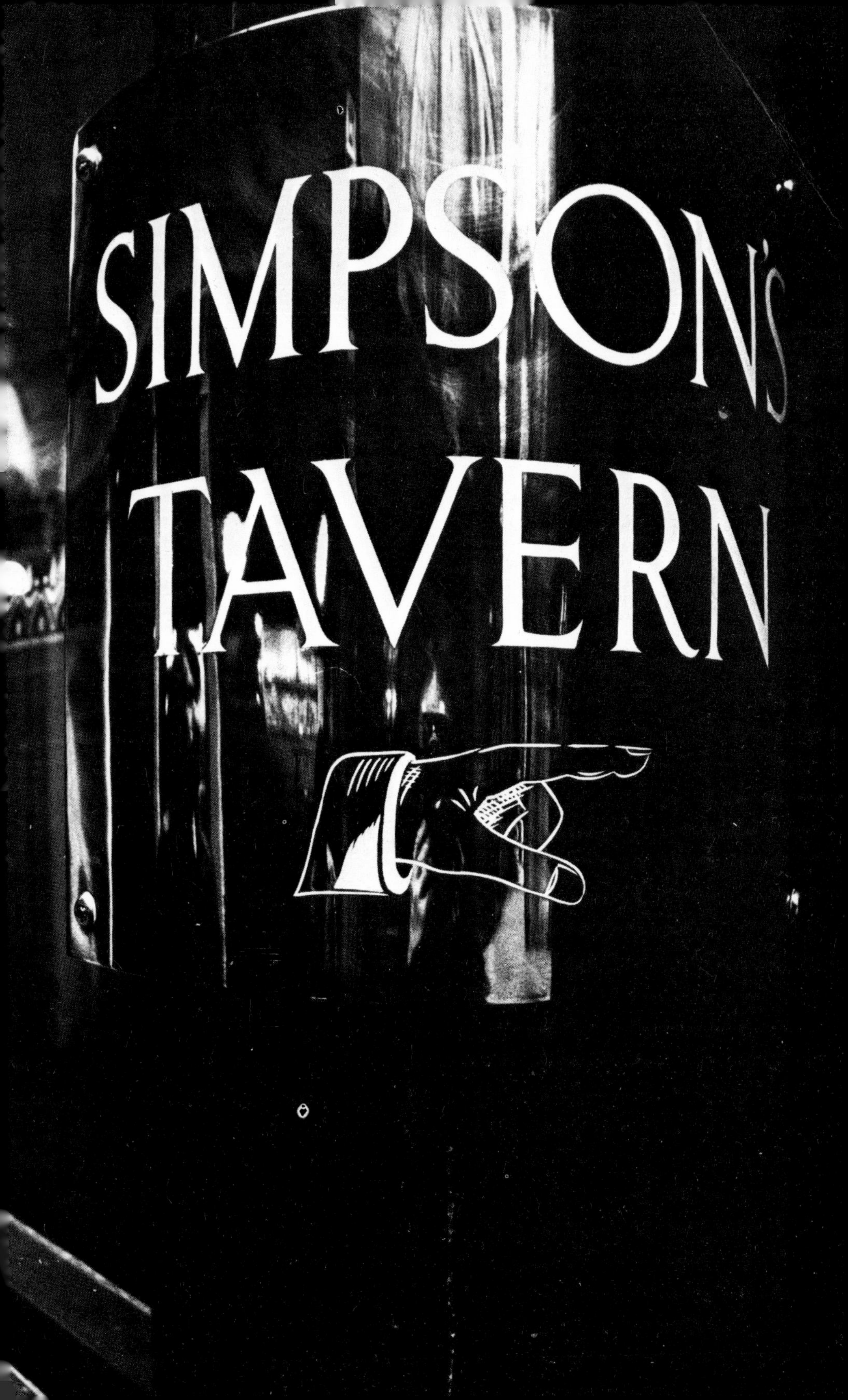
SIMPSON'S
TAVERN

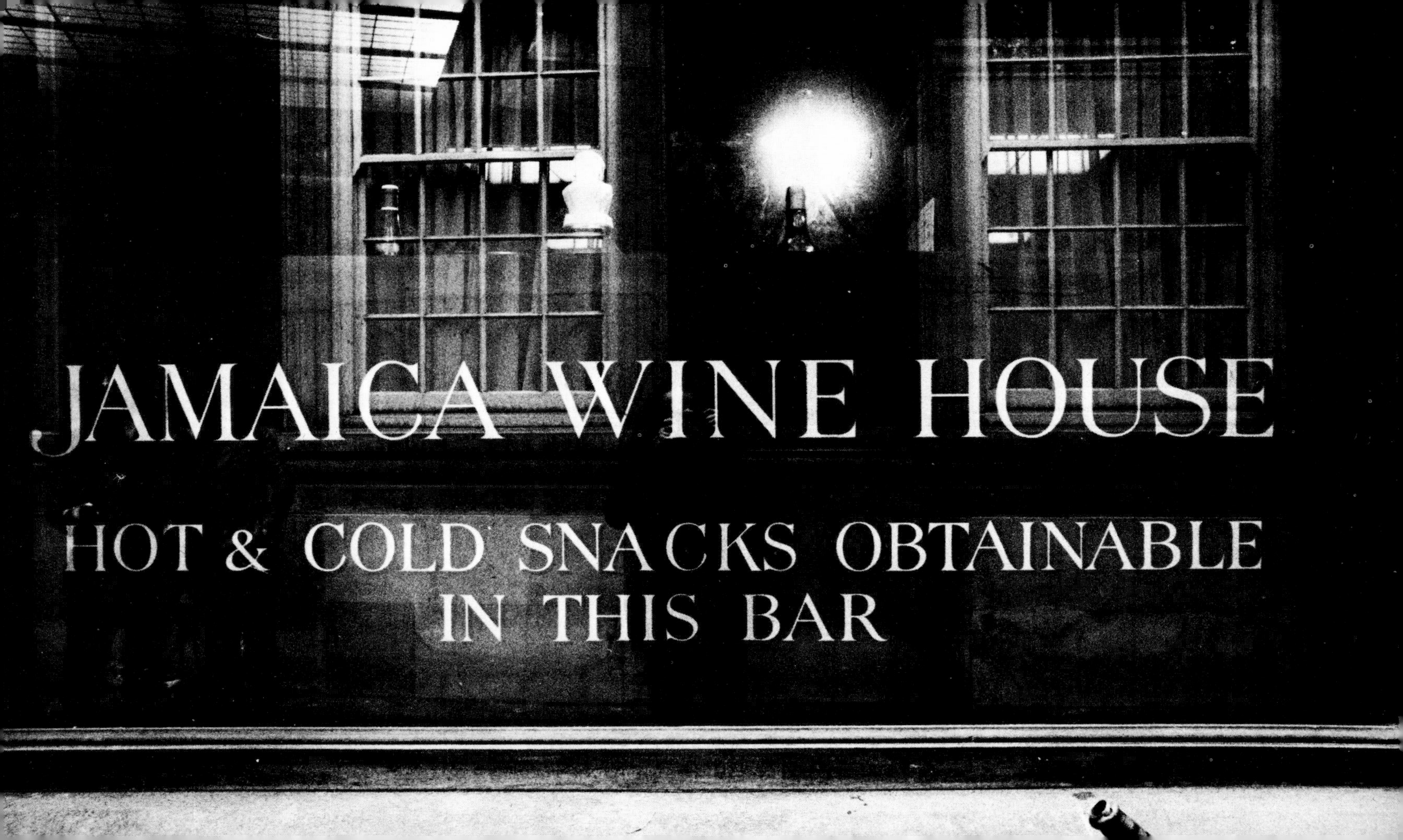
JAMAICA WINE HOUSE
HOT & COLD SNACKS OBTAINABLE
IN THIS BAR

The PORTER Has Orders To
Prevent Old Clothes Men & Others
From Calling Articles For Sale, Also
To Prevent Children Playing &c.
No Horses Allowed Within This Inn

Staples Inn

The Salisbury, St. Martin's Lane

Jamaica Wine House

Red Lion, Duke of York Street

The Salisbury

Jamaica Wine House

Soho

Bolt Court

St. Michael's Court

Regent's Park

Turret Bookshop

Portobello Road

Notting Hill

your travel agent and the British Travel Authority Hotel and Restaurant Guide.

If you still can't make up your mind, then take a package tour. You'll stay where you're put.

And if you don't like the hotel once you get there, or if you ignore my advice and hop over on the spur of the moment with nowhere to sleep, look under Help! and Tourist/Travel Services.

Law

THE LEGAL PROFESSION not only occupies some of the best-preserved real estate in London but also provides some of her best free entertainment. English lawyers come in two varieties: solicitors, who handle the bulk of every day legal work, and barristers, who argue cases in court. Their respective governing bodies are:

THE LAW SOCIETY, 113 Chancery Lane, W.C.2 (242-1222).

GENERAL COUNCIL OF THE BAR, Carp Mael Building, Temple, E.C.4. (Information: 4a Essex Court, E.C.4 [353-2261].)

Both are courteous and helpful in answering visitors' inquiries. Given sufficient warning, they will also arrange conducted tours for small groups. Alternatively, permission to see inside the halls, chapels and other private buildings of the four Inns of Court can normally be had on application to their respective Treasury Officers:

INNER TEMPLE, E.C.4 (353-7211).

MIDDLE TEMPLE, E.C.4 (353-4973).

LINCOLN'S INN, Chancery Lane, W.C.2 (405-1393).

GRAY'S INN, Gray's Inn Road, W.C.1 (242-8591).

COURTS

ROYAL COURTS OF JUSTICE (Law Courts), Strand, W.C.2.
Open 10:30 am to 4 pm (when Courts are in recess). When the Courts are sitting, the public gallery is open from 10:30 am to 1 pm; and from 2 pm till the Courts rise.

OLD BAILEY (Central Criminal Court), Newgate, E.C.4.
Stands on the site of the notorious Newgate Prison. Famous for criminal trials.
Open—when the courts are sitting, public gallery is open 10 am to 1 pm; 2 pm till the courts rise. Parties are shown around the building on Saturdays at approximately 11 am.

LAW COLLECTIONS

PUBLIC RECORD OFFICE, Chancery Lane, W.C.2 (405-0741).
Statutes and archives from the 11th century onwards. *Open Mondays to Fridays 1 pm to 4 pm.*

THE BRITISH MUSEUM, Great Russell Street, W.C.1.
Department of State Papers.

Media

DEPRIVED AMERICANS tend to lose their heads when faced with a choice of 11 daily papers and seven Sunday papers and insist on *The Herald Tribune*, printed in Paris and sold on most London newsstands. Not surprisingly, it carries mostly American material, including *The New York Times* crossword puzzle and Wall Street's closing prices. But for old times' sake, try choosing among papers again:

MORNING NEWSPAPERS

The Times. (Literate, moderate, top people's paper.)

The Guardian. (Literate, progressive, intelligent.)

The Financial Times. (A readable *Wall Street Journal.*)

The Daily Telegraph. (High Tory, often pompous and reactionary.)

The Daily Express. (Popular, splashy, flag-waver.)

The Sun. (Brisk, flashy tabloid.)

The Daily Mirror. (See *Sun.*)

The Daily Mail. (See *Mirror.*)

The Morning Star. (Fairly independent Communist paper.)

AFTERNOON NEWSPAPERS

The Evening News. (Untidy, working-class Tory paper.)

The Evening Standard. (Slick tabloid, best London coverage.)

SUNDAY NEWSPAPERS

The Sunday Times. (Sister to *The Times.*)

The Observer. (Spiritual sister to *The Guardian.*)

The Sunday Telegraph. (Like the daily.)

The Sunday Express. (Like the daily.)

The People. (Simple-minded exposés, progressive, working-class.)

News of the World. (Sex and Tory politics.)
The Sunday Mirror. (See daily.)

NEWSPAPER TOURS

News of the World, 30 Bouverie Street, E.C.4 (353-3030).
  *Tours every Saturday night, except on public holidays and
  bank holiday weekends, at 7 pm, 7:15 pm, 7:30 pm, 8 pm,
  8:15 pm, 8:30 pm, 9 pm, 9:15 pm, 9:30 pm, 10 pm, 10:15 pm,
  and 10:30 pm.*

Sun, 30 Bouverie Street, E.C.4 (583-9100 extension 221).
  *Tours take place from Monday to Friday at 8:45 pm, 9:15
  pm, 9:45 pm, 10:15 pm and 10:45 pm.*
  Each tour lasts about an hour. Children must be seven or
  over and accompanied by an adult.

MAGAZINES

As in the States, the general consumer magazines are going
or gone, but the newsstands are busting out all over with
specialist journals of all sorts. These are very English:

New Statesman
Punch
Countryman
Harpers/Queen
Nova
Private Eye

And don't forget to pick up your copies of *Time Out* and
What's On.

TELEVISION AND RADIO

Television Channels:
  BBC 1
  BBC 2
  ITV
Radio Channels:
  Radio 1: *247m AM (pop)*
  Radio 2: *1500m AM, 89.1 MHz FM (light)*
  Radio 3: *464m AM, 194 MHz FM (classical)*
  Radio 4: *320m AM, 93.5 MHz FM (talk)*
  Radio London: *95.3 MHz FM (local)*
Daily Press, Radio Times and TV Times for program details.

TICKETS

Write to the following for tickets to radio and television audience shows:

Ticket Unit, BBC, London W1A AA (radio and television).

Ticket Office, Thames Television, Television House, 306 Euston Road, N.W.1.

Ticket Office, London Weekend Television, Station House, Harrow Road, Wembley, Middlesex.

TOURS

ITA Television Gallery, 70 Brompton Road, S.W.3 (584-7011). Ninety-minute tour which explains the history of television, how programs are produced, etc.

Tours commence: 10 am, 11:30 am, 2:30 pm and 4 pm.

Museums

THERE ARE HUNDREDS OF THEM. The usual tourist circuit takes in just the blockbusters:

BRITISH MUSEUM, Great Russell Street, W.C.1 (636-1555).
10 am to 5 pm (Sunday 2:30 pm to 6 pm).

VICTORIA & ALBERT MUSEUM, Cromwell Road, S.W.1 (589-6371).
Fine and applied arts.
10 am to 6 pm (Sunday 2:30 pm to 6 pm).

NATURAL HISTORY MUSEUM, Cromwell Road, S.W.1 (589-6323).
10 am to 6 pm (Sunday 2:30 pm to 6 pm).

SCIENCE MUSEUM, Exhibition Road, S.W.7 (589-6371).
10 am to 6 pm (Sunday 2:30 pm to 6 pm).

IMPERIAL WAR MUSEUM, Lambeth Road, S.E.1 (735-8922).
10 am to 6 pm (Sunday 2 pm to 6 pm).

MADAME TUSSAUD'S (and Planetarium), Marylebone Road, N.W.1 (935-6861).
10 am to 5:30 pm (Saturday, Sunday 10 am to 6:30 pm).

After that, visitors can take their pick of the specialized collections. These are a few of the best:

ARTILLERY MUSEUM, The Rotunda, Woolwich Common, S.E.18 (854-2424).
Muskets, guns and field pieces.
10 am to 12:45 pm and 2 pm to 5 pm (Sunday 2 pm to 5 pm).

BRITISH PIANO MUSEUM, 368 High Street, Brentwood, Middlesex (near Kew Bridge). (560-8108).
Old pianos and other musical instruments.
Guided tour and demonstration.
Donation 20p.
March to November, Saturday and Sunday 2:30 pm to 5:30 pm.

BRITISH THEATRE MUSEUM, Leighton House, 12 Holland Park Road, W.14 (937-3052).

British theater from the 18th century on.
Tuesday, Thursday, Saturday 11 am to 5 pm.
(Also Leighton House Art Gallery and Museum).

CHARTERED INSURANCE INSTITUTE'S MUSEUM, 20 Aldermanbury, E.C.2 (606-3835).
Collection of insurance companies' fire marks, also fire-fighting equipment.
9:15 am to 5:15 pm. Closed Saturday and Sunday.

CLOCK MUSEUM (adjoining Guildhall Library), King Street, Cheapside, E.C.2.
Monday to Friday 9:30 am to 5 pm.
Saturday 9:30 am to 12 pm and 2 pm to 5 pm.

DICKENS' HOUSE, 48 Doughty Street, W.C.1 (405-2127).
Many personal relics.
Headquarters of the Dickens Fellowship.
Admission 15p.
Monday to Saturday 10 am to 5 pm.

EMBROIDERERS GUILD, 73 Wimpole Street, W.1 (935-3281).
Unusual collection of embroidery.
Telephone for hours of viewing.

GEFFRYE MUSEUM, Kingsland Road, Shoreditch, E.2 (739-8368).
18th-century almshouses.
Series of period furnished rooms from 1600 onwards.
Tuesday to Saturday 10 am to 5 pm.
Sunday 2 pm to 5 pm.

GOLDSMITHS' HALL, Foster Lane, E.C.2 (606-8971).
Modern silver and jewelry and fine collection of antique plate.
By appointment.

GORDON MEDICAL MUSEUM, St. Thomas' Street, S.E.1 (407-7600).
Models and specimens dealing with human diseases.
By appointment.

GUARDS' MUSEUM, Wellington Barracks, Birdcage Walk, S.W.1.
Models, relics, uniforms and weapons.
Temporarily housed in the Guardroom beside the Chapel.
Admission 5p.
Monday to Saturday 10 am to 5 pm.
Sunday 11:30 am to 1:30 pm and 2:30 pm to 5 pm.
Closes 4 pm in the winter.

JEWISH MUSEUM, Woburn House, Upper Woburn Place, W.C.1 (387-3081).
Collection of world Judaica.
Monday to Thursday 2:30 pm to 5 pm.
Friday and Sunday 10:30 am to 12:45 pm.
Closed Saturdays, Jewish holy days, bank holidays.

LONDON MUSEUM, Kensington Palace, Kensington Gardens, W.8 937-9816).
History and social life of London from Roman times to present.
March to September 10 am to 6 pm, October to February 10 am to 4 pm.
Sunday from 2 pm.

LONDON SILVER VAULTS, Chancery House, Southampton Buildings, Chancery Lane, W.C.2 (242-3844).
Art in silverware.
Also objets d'art of ivory, jade and enamel, and English china.
Monday to Friday 9 am to 5:30 pm.
Saturday 9 am to 12:30 pm.

LORD'S CRICKET MUSEUM, Lord's Cricket Ground, St. John's Wood, N.W.8 (289-1615).
The history of cricket.
10:30 am to 4 pm (or close of play).
Out of season, Monday to Friday 10 am to 4 pm.
Admission 5p.

MUSEUM OF BRITISH TRANSPORT, Clapham High Street, S.W.4 (622-3241).
Historic locomotives, royal coaches, streetcars and buses.
Monday to Saturday 10 am to 5:30 pm.
Closed Sunday.
Admission 15p.

MUSIC BOX GALLERY, 81 George Street, Portman Square, W.1.
Antique music boxes, clocks and singing birds in cages.
Craftsmen to help with repairs.
Monday to Friday 9:30 am to 5:30 pm.
Saturday by appointment.

NATIONAL MARITIME MUSEUM, Romney Road, S.E.10 (858-4422).
Ship models, charts, navigational equipment, etc.
10 am to 6 pm (Sunday 2:30 pm to 6 pm).

NATIONAL POSTAL MUSEUM, King Edward Street, E.C.1 (432-3851).
Most valuable collection of its type in the world.
Reference Library.
Monday to Saturday 10:30 am to 4:30 pm.

OPERATING THEATRE, Old St. Thomas's Hospital, St. Thomas's Street, Southward, S.E.1.
A semi-circular operating theater which lay concealed for 50 years and is now a museum.
Monday, Wednesday, Friday 12:30 pm to 4 pm.
Entrance by Chapter House.

PHARMACEUTICAL SOCIETY'S MUSEUM, 17 Bloomsbury Square, W.C.1 (405-8967).
Drugs and apparatus. *By appointment.*

PIPE MUSEUM, DUNHILL'S, 30 Duke Street, S.W.1 (493-9161).
Particularly fine collection of clay pipes, inter alia.
Monday to Friday 9:30 am to 5:30 pm.
Saturday 9:30 am to 1 pm.

POLLOCK'S TOY MUSEUM, 1 Scala Street, W.1 (636-3452).
Unique collection of toy theaters and toys.
Monday to Saturday 10 am to 5 pm.
Admission 10p.

ROYAL MEWS, Buckingham Palace Road, S.W.1 (930-4832).
Queen's horses and royal equipage.
Wednesday and Thursday 2 pm to 4 pm.

THEATRE MUSEUM, 5 Venner Road, Sydenham, S.E.19.
One of the most comprehensive theater collections in Britain.
By written appointment only.

WELLCOME HISTORICAL MEDICAL MUSEUM, 183 Euston Road, N.W.1 (387-4477).
History of medicine.
Monday to Friday 10 am to 5 pm.
Saturday 9:30 am to 4:30 pm.

Music

The Musical Times, The Times on Saturday, The Observer on Sunday, Time Out and What's On have their work cut out trying to keep up with London's hyperactive musical life, particularly in the winter. Most of it centers around the following halls:

THE ROYAL FESTIVAL HALL, South Bank, S.E.1 (928-3191).

THE ROYAL ALBERT HALL, Kensington Gore, S.W.7 (589-8212).

QUEEN ELIZABETH HALL, South Bank, S.E.1 (928-3191).

ST. PANCRAS TOWN HALL, Euston Road, N.W.1 (278-4444).

THE WIGMORE HALL, 36 Wigmore Street, W.1 (935-2141).

PURCELL ROOM, South Bank, S.E.1 (928-3191).

Interesting things also happen at Bishopsgate Hall in the City; St. John's, Smith Square, S.W.1; the Victoria & Albert Museum, S.W. 7; the Royal Academy of Music, N.W.1; the Royal College of Music, S.W.7 and the Law Society's Hall, W.C.2—so keep an eye open for these.

Opera and dance are centered on:

ROYAL OPERA HOUSE, Covent Garden, W.C.2 (240-1066).

SADLERS WELLS OPERA COMPANY, Coliseum, W.C.2 (836-3161).

SADLERS WELLS THEATRE, Rosebery Avenue, E.C.1 (837-1672). (Visiting companies.)

LONDON CONTEMPORARY DANCE COMPANY, The Place Theatre, Dukes Road, W.C.1 (387-0161).

BALLET RAMBERT, 31 Pembridge Road, W.11 (727-5700).

LONDON'S FESTIVAL BALLET, 48 Welbeck Street, W.1 (486-3337).

MUSIC CLUBS

LONDON MUSICAL CLUB, 21 Holland Park, W.1 (727-4440). Frequent concerts, recitals, meetings and discussions for members. Facilities for rehearsal and practice.

Music Club of London, 36 Nottingham Place, W.1 (486-4116). Organizes visits to places of musical interest, operas, concerts etc. Some events open to non-members.

The Musical Times is the best source of information on organ recitals, choral and church music.

$\mathcal{N}$ightlife

LONDONERS HAVE BEEN WASTING their substance in riotous living for 2,000 years, so they're quite good at it now. *Time Out*, *What's On* and the daily papers cover respectable places quite thoroughly; hotel porters, taxi-drivers and Soho corner loiterers are usually well-informed about the other kind (especially when you cross their palms with banknotes). These are the places mentioned in the text, plus a few extra for luck:

NIGHT CLUBS (members only, so take passports)

ASTOR CLUB, Berkeley Square, W.1 (499-3181).

BLUE ANGEL, 14 Berkeley Street, W.1 (629-1443).

CHURCHILL'S, 160 New Bond Street, W.1 (493-2626).

DANNY LA RUE'S, 17 Hanover Square, W.1 (499-4203).

EMBASSY, 6-8 Old Bond Street, W.1 (493-5275).

EVE, 189 Regent Street, W.1 (734-0557).

NELL GWYNNE, 69 Dean Street, W.1 (437-3886).

RONNIE SCOTT'S, 47 Frith Street, W.1 (437-4239).

21 CLUB, 8 Chesterfield Gardens, W.1 (499-3233).

DISCOTHÈQUES (members only; passports again)

ANNABEL'S, 44 Hays Mews, W.1 (629-3558).

BAG O'NAILS, 9 Kingly Street, W.1 (734-0953).

BUMPERS, Coventry Street, W.1 (734-5600). Non-membership.

HATCHETT'S, 67a Piccadilly, W.1 (493-1871). Non-membership.

MARQUEE, 90 Wardour Street, W.1 (437-2375).

RAFFLES, 287 King's Road, S.W.3 (352-1091).

SADDLE ROOM, 1a Hamilton Mews, W.1 (499-4994).

SPEAKEASY, 48 Margaret Street, W.1 (580-8810).

TIFFANY'S, 22 Shaftesbury Avenue, W.1 (437-5012). Non-membership.

TRAMP, 40 Jermyn Street, W.1 (734-0565).

DINNER/DANCE

BARRACUDA, 1 Baker Street, W.1 (486-2724).

QUAGLINO'S, 16 Bury Street, W.1 (930-6767).

SAVOY HOTEL, Strand, W.C.2 (836-4343).

TIBERIO, 22 Queen Street, W.1 (629-3561).

VILLA DEI CESARI, 135 Grosvenor Road, S.W.1 (828-7453).

CASINOS (membership plus 48-hour wait, so call early)

CLERMONT CLUB, 44 Berkeley Square, W.1 (499-6522).

CROCKFORD'S, 16 Carlton House Terrace, S.W.1 (930-2721).

CURZON HOUSE, 21 Curzon Street, W.1 (629-0164).

INTERNATIONAL SPORTING CLUB, Berkeley Square, W.1 (629-1657).

PALM BEACH, 30 Berkeley Street, W.1 (493-6585).

PLAYBOY CLUB, 45 Park Lane, W.1 (629-6666).

VICTORIA SPORTING CLUB, 150-162 Edgware Road, W.2 (262-2467).

JAZZ CLUBS

RONNIE SCOTT'S, 47 Frith Street, W.1 (437-4239).

COLYER CLUB, 10-11 Great Newport Street, W.C.2.

THE 100 CLUB, 100 Oxford Street, W.1.

STRIP JOINTS (Membership)

CARNIVAL, 12 Old Compton Street, W.1 (437-8337).

CASINO DE PARIS, 5 Denman Street, W.1 (437-2872).

SUNSET STRIP, 30 Dean Street, W.1.

BEST BARS

BROWN'S HOTEL, Dover Street, W.1.

CONNAUGHT HOTEL, Carlos Place, W.1.

JULES'S BAR, 85 Jermyn Street, W.1.

RITZ, RIVOLI BAR, Piccadilly, W.1.

SAVOY, AMERICAN BAR, Strand, W.C.2.

WESTBURY, POLO BAR, New Bond Street, W.1.

$\mathcal{N}umber\ \mathcal{P}lease$

ALL-NIGHT RESTAURANTS

CAVENDISH HOTEL, Ribblesdale Room, Jermyn Street, S.W.1 (930-2111).

GROSVENOR HOUSE, La Piazza Buttery, Park Lane, W.1 (499-6363).

LONDONDERRY HOUSE, Pelican, Park Lane, W.1 (493-7292).

BABYSITTERS

Solve Your Problem, 25a Kensington Church Street, W.8 (937-0906).

BEDTIME STORY *Dial 246-8000 after 6 pm.*

CLEANERS AND LAUNDRY

COLLINS, 317 Regent Street, W.1 (636-5152).

Other branches around London.

JEEVES, 8 Pont Street, S.W.1 (235-1101).

CLOTHES, RENTAL

MOSS BROS., Bedford Street, W.C.2 (240-4567).

DIAL-A-DISC *Dial 160 between 6 pm and 8 pm.*

DIAL-A-POEM *Dial 836-2872.*

ESCORTS

NORMAN COURTNEY GUIDE & ESCORT SERVICES, 37 Old Bond Street, W.1 (493-5073).

THE CARLTON TEAM, 5 South Molton Street, W.1 (493-0202).

FLOWERS

FLOWER SERVICES, 2 Carlos Place, W.1 (629-0932).

FOOT COMFORT

SCHOLL's, 59 Brompton Road, S.W.3 (589-1887).
254 Regent Street, W.1 (734-3583).
J. MOCK & SONS, 1 Warwick Street, W.1 (437-4497).

HELICOPTER

RENT-A-COPTER, 2 Lowndes Street, S.W.1 (235-6477).

INTERPRETERS

LONDON VISITORS and INTERPRETER SERVICE, 175 Piccadilly, W.1 (493-1900).

LAUNDRY AND CLEANERS See Cleaners and Laundry.

LEGAL AID

American tourists are advised to contact the U.S. Embassy, 24 Grosvenor Square, W.1 (499-9000).

LOST PROPERTY

BUS/TUBE: London Transport Lost Property Office, 200 Baker Street, N.W.1.

TRAIN: Main line terminus.

TAXI: Lost Property Office, Penton Street, N.1.

AIR TRAVEL: Lost property held by each individual airline. If lost in main airport buildings, then inquire at British Airport Police, Lost Property Office, Heathrow, Middlesex (759-4321).

ELSEWHERE: Local police station.

MEAL DELIVERY SERVICE

DIAL-A-MEAL, 173 Knightsbridge, S.W.7 (584-9111).

MESSENGER SERVICE

Call the Post Office at 606-9876 and they will explain how to get a messenger. If it sounds too complicated, look up a commercial service in the Yellow Pages or give whatever it is to a cab driver to deliver.

MINI - CABS (chauffeur driven cars): 24-hour service.

CENTRAL LONDON GROUP (778-0201).

SOUTH LONDON GROUP (778-2233).

MINI-CABS (KENSINGTON) (370-2371).

MINI-CABS (KNIGHTSBRIDGE) (589-7755).

MINI-CABS (ISLINGTON) (837-0221).

RADIO TAXIS 24-hour service. Will also collect, deliver etc.

OWNER DRIVERS RADIO TAXI SERVICE, 144 Shireland Road, W.9 (289-1133).

RECIPE FOR THE DAY Dial 246-8071

SECRETARIAL SERVICE

AUTO-SEC, 404 Lea Bridge Road, E.10 (539-8332).

24-hour 'phone dictation service.

STOCK PRICES

FINANCIAL TIMES SHARE INDEX—246-8026. (London Stock Exchange.)

AMERICAN STOCK EXCHANGES:

Arvid C. Willen, Merrill, Lynch, Pierce, Fenner & Smith (499-3550).

TIME Dial 123

TRAFFIC INFORMATION

For road and traffic conditions within 50 miles of London, dial 246-8021.

WAKE-UP SERVICE Dial 191

WEATHER

Weather forecast for London 246-8091.

For personal service, call the London Weather Center (836-4311).

Parks and Gardens

NOBODY GOES TO LONDON FOR A SUNTAN, but it could happen. Fine weather is finer there than in other cities, partly because the air is cleaner but mostly because there's somewhere to go —the parks. The Greater London Council publishes a 104-page book every year just to list what goes on there (officially, that is—Londoners also improvise a lot). And if you like walking in the rain . . . these are some of the best:

ST. JAMES'S PARK, Westminster, S.W.1.
Oldest Royal Park, acquired in 1532. Redesigned in the 1820's by John Nash. Bird sanctuary, bandstand and marvelous views (93 acres).

BUSHY PARK, Teddington, Middlesex.
Noted for its deer. Wren designed the Chestnut Avenue which runs from Hampton Court Gate to Teddington Gate (1,099 acres).

GREEN PARK, Westminster, S.W.1.
Well-wooded parkland (53 acres).

GREENWICH PARK, Greenwich, S.W.10.
Home of the Royal Observatory, Royal Naval College and Maritime Museum. Also 13 acres of natural woodland for birds and deer (approx. 200 acres).

HOLLAND PARK, Kensington, W.8.
Secluded gardens with peacocks and 28 acres of woodland (54 acres).

HAMPSTEAD HEATH, Hampstead, N.W.3.
High and hilly land connecting with Parliament Hill, Kenwood and Golder's Hill; ponds for swimming and fishing, kite flying (800 acres).

KEW GARDENS, Surrey.
World famous botanical gardens with practically every

known species of flowers, trees and hot-house plants (300 acres).

LINCOLN'S INN FIELDS, Holborn, W.C.2.
Gardens, netball and tennis courts (7 acres).

WATERLOW PARK, N.6.
The house where Nell Gwynne lived, plus ponds, tennis courts, summer open-air theater and aviary. Pass through to Highgate Cemetery (26 acres).

WIMBLEDON COMMON, S.W. 19.
Famous old windmill, wooded parkland, heath and lakes (1,000 acres).

HAMPTON COURT PARK, Hampton Court, Middlesex.
South of Bushy Park, Hampton Court is the formal park of the great Tudor palace. Flower gardens. The Great Vine, planted in 1769. The Maze, planted during Queen Anne's reign (676 acres).

HYDE PARK, W.1.
Rotten Row for horse riding; the Serpentine for mixed swimming, boating and fishing; Speaker's Corner (361 acres).

KENSINGTON GARDENS, W.2.
Adjoining Hyde Park. Kensington Palace, the Albert Memorial and Peter Pan's statue. Good children's playground, kite flying, Round Pond for sailing model boats (275 acres).

PRIMROSE HILL, N.W.3.
Fine views over London, 200 ft. up (62 acres).

REGENT'S PARK, N.W.1.
Designed by Nash. Queen Mary's Rose Garden, Open-Air Theatre, the Zoological Gardens, Regents Canal and boating lake (472 acres).

RICHMOND PARK, Richmond, Surrey.
Natural open parkland with herds of red and fallow deer, ancient oaks, ponds, enclosed forestry plantations and abun-

dant wild life. White Lodge is now the home of the Royal Ballet School (2,500 acres).

BATTERSEA PARK, S.W.11.

Scaled down Coney Island, plus a lake, deerpark and miniature railway (200 acres).

$\mathcal{P}ubs$

THERE'S NO ACCOUNTING FOR TASTE. If you like the way it feels, it's a good pub. If you don't, somebody else does, and you're left with only about 7,000 others to choose from. Opening hours are, on weekdays, 11 or 11:30 am to 3 pm and 5 or 5:30 pm to 11 pm, and on Sundays, noon till 2 pm and 7 pm to 10:30 pm. But be careful with City of London pubs. Most of them are closed on weekends. All these are mentioned in the text and essentially likable:

ANCHOR, 1 Bankside, S.E.1

ANGEL, 21 Rotherhithe Street, S.E. 16

ANTELOPE, 22 Eaton Terrace, S.E.1

AUDLEY, 41 Mount Street, W.1

BLACK CAP, 171 Camden High Street, N.W.1

BLACK FRIAR, 174 Queen Victoria Street, E.C.4

BULL'S HEAD, 373 Lonsdale Road, S.W. 13

BUNCH OF GRAPES, Shepherd Market, W.1

BUNCH OF GRAPES, 207 Brompton Road, S.W.3

CHELSEA POTTER, 119 King's Road, S.W.3

CHESHIRE CHEESE, 145 Fleet Street, E.C.4

CITY ARMS, 1 West Ferry Road, E.14

FINCH'S, 190 Fulham Road, S.W.10

FLASK, 77 West Hill, Highgate, N.6

GEORGE, 77 Borough High Street, S.E.1

GRENADIER, 18 Wilton Row, S.W.1

HORN TAVERN, 29 Knightrider Street, E.C.4

IRON BRIDGE TAVERN, 447 East India Dock Road, E.14

JAMAICA WINE BAR, St. Michael's Alley, Cornhill, E.C.3

LAMB & FLAG, 33 Rose Street, Covent Garden, W.C.2

MAYFLOWER, 117 Rotherhithe Street, S.E.16

NEW MERLIN'S CAVE, Margery Street, W.C.1

OLD BELL TAVERN, 95 Fleet Street, E.C.4

OLD MITRE, 1 Ely Court, Ely Place, E.C.1

OLD WINE SHADES, Martin Lane, E.C.4

PAXTON'S HEAD, 153 Knightsbridge, S.W.1

PHOENIX, 37 Cavendish Square, W.1

PROSPECT OF WHITBY, 57 Wapping Wall, E.1

RED LION, 1 Waverton Street, W.1

RED LION, 2 Duke of York Street, W.1

SALISBURY, 90 St. Martin's Lane, W.C.2

SAMUEL PEPYS, Brooks Wharf, Upper Thames Street, E.C.4

SHERLOCK HOLMES, 10 Northumberland Street, W.C.2

SPANIARDS INN, Spaniards Road, N.W.3

TALLY HO, Fortress Road, Kentish Town, N.W.5

TOWN OF RAMSGATE, 62 Wapping High Street, E.1

TRAFALGAR, 200 King's Road, S.W.3

WATERMAN'S ARMS, 1 Glengarnock Avenue, E.14

WIDOW'S SON, 75 Devons Road, E.3

And if you don't want to take my word for it, ask THE PUB INFORMATION BUREAU, 333 Vauxhall Bridge Road, S.W.1 (828-3261).

Religion

VISITORS WHO WANT TO FIND OUT where their co-religionists practice their faith in London should check the following list. If their religion or sect isn't mentioned, chances are they're on their own—although the Church of England Inquiry Center (222-9011) might be ecumenical enough to advise them.

BAPTIST UNION, 4 Southampton Row, W.C.1 (405-2045).

BUDDHIST SOCIETY, 58 Eccleston Square, S.W.1 (828-1313).

CHRISTIAN SCIENTIST, Ingersoll House, 9 Kingsway, W.C.2 (836-2808).

CHURCH OF SCOTLAND, St. Columba's Church of Scotland Office, Pont Street, S.W.1 (584-2321).

CONGREGATIONAL CHURCH, Livingstone House, 11 Carteret Street, S.W.1 (930-0061).

FREE CHURCH FEDERAL COUNCIL, 27 Tavistock Square, W.C.1 (387-8413).

GREEK ORTHODOX, 5 Craven Hill, W.2 (723-4787).

THE HINDU CENTRE, 39 Grafton Terrace, N.W.5 (485-8200).

ISLAMIC CULTURAL CENTRE & LONDON CENTRAL MOSQUE, 146 Park Road, N.W.8 (723-7611).

JEHOVAH'S WITNESSES, Watch Tower House, The Ridgeway, N.W.7 (959-6773).

BOARD OF DEPUTIES OF BRITISH JEWS, Woburn House, Upper Woburn Place, W.C.1 (387-3952).

LUTHERAN COUNCIL, 8 Collingham Gardens, S.W.5 (373-1141).

METHODIST CHURCH INFORMATION SERVICE, Room 73, 1 Central Buildings, Central Hall, Westminister, S.W.1 (930-1751).

PENTECOSTAL CHURCHES (Assemblies of God), 30 Blomfield Villas, W.2 (286-9261).

PRESBYTERIAN CHURCH, 86 Tavistock Place, W.C.1 (837-0862).

QUAKERS, Friends Home Service Committee, Friends House, Euston Road, N.W.1 (387-3601).

ROMAN CATHOLIC, Catholic Central Library and Information Centre, 47 Francis Street, S.W.1 (834-6128).

SALVATION ARMY, 101 Queen Victoria Street, E.C.4 (236-5222).

SEVENTH DAY ADVENTISTS, 123 Regent Street, W.1 (734-8888).

SPIRITUALIST ASSOCIATION, 33 Belgrave Square, S.W.1 (235-3351).

UNITARIAN CHURCHES, Essex Hall, Essex Street, W.C.2 (240-2384).

```
┌──────────────────────────────────────────────────┐
│                                                    │
│                                                    │
│   Restaurants                                      │
│                                                    │
│                                                    │
└──────────────────────────────────────────────────┘
```

WHO NEEDS A CHOICE of 5,000 restaurants for dinner? How many meals can you eat in a week or two anyway?

If you take food seriously, you can't go wrong with a reservation at any of these:

TEN OF THE BEST EXPENSIVE RESTAURANTS

CAPRICE, Arlington Street, S.W.1 (493-6294) French/International

ETOILE, 30 Charlotte Street, W.1 (636-7189) French

LE GRAND VEFOUR, Chesham Place, S.W.1 (235-3151) French

MIRABELLE, 56 Curzon Street, W.1 (499-4636) French/International

MISTER CHOW, 151 Knightsbridge, S.W.1 (589-7347) Chinese (Pekinese)

PARKES (BENSON'S), 4 Beauchamp Place, S.W.3 (589-1390) Orignal

PRUNIERS, 72 St. James Street, S.W.1 (493-1373) French/Fish

TIBERIO, 22 Queen Street, W.1 (629-3561) Italian

WHITE TOWER, Percy Street, W.1 (636-8141) Greek

WILTONS, 27 Bury Street, S.W.1 (930-8391) English/International

TEN OF THE BEST MODERATELY PRICED RESTAURANTS

BROMPTON GRILL, 243 Brompton Road, S.W.3 (589-8005) French

DUMPLING INN, 15a Gerrard Street, W.1 (437-2567) Chinese (Pekinese)

HUNGRY HORSE, 196 Fulham Road, S.W.10 (352-8081) English
KEBAB HOUSE, 56 Maple Street, W.1 (636-0932) Greek
LE FRANCAIS, 259 Fulham Road, S.W.3 (352-3668) French
NICK'S DINER, 88 Ifield Road, S.W. 10 (352-5641) International
SAN LORENZO, 22 Beauchamp Place, S.W.3 (584-1074) Italian
SAN MARTINO, 103 Walton Street, S.W.3 (589-3833) Italian
TANDOORI, 153 Fulham Road, S.W.3 (589-7617) North Indian
WHEELER'S, 19 Old Compton Street, W.1 (437-7661) Fish

OTHER GOOD RESTAURANTS MENTIONED IN THE TEXT ARE:

ALVARO'S, 124 King's Road, S.W.3 (589-6296) Italian
BILL BENTLEY'S, 31 Beauchamp Place, S.W.3 (589-5080) Fish
BIRCH'S, 3 Angel Court, E.C.2 (606-0602) English. Lunch only.
CARRIER'S, 2 Camden Passage, N.1 (226-5353) Original
COQ D'OR, Stratton House, Stratton Street, W.1 (629-7807) French
EMBERSON'S, 5b Shepherd Street, W.1 (499-1906) Fish
EMPRESS, 15 Berkeley Street, W.1 (629-6126) French/International
GALLERY RENDEZVOUS, 53 Beak Street, W.1 (734-0445) Pekinese
GEALE'S, 2 Farmer Street, W.8 (727-7969) Fish and chips.
GEORGE & VULTURE, 3 Castle Court, E.C.3 (626-9710) English. (Lunch only).
GREAT AMERICAN DISASTER, 335 Fulham Road, S.W.10 (351-1188) American
HARD ROCK CAFE, Piccadilly, W.1 (629-0382) American
INIGO JONES, 14 Garrick Street, W.C.2 (836-6456) International
LEE HO FOOK, 15 Gerrard Street, W.1 (734-8929) Cantonese
MERIDIANA, 169 Fulham Road, S.W.3 (589-8815) Italian
PIZZA EXPRESS, 30 Coptic Street, W.C.1 (636-3232)
SAN FREDIANO, 62 Fulham Road, S.W.3 (584-8375) Italian
SCOTT'S, 20 Mount Street, W.1 (629-5248) French
SIMPSON'S TAVERN, 38½ Cornhill, E.C.3 (626-8901) English. (Lunch only).

TERRAZZA, 19 Romilly Street, W.1 (437-8991) Italian

WHITE HOUSE, Albany Street, N.W.1 (387-1200) French/International

And if you're still hungry, work your way through *The Good Food Guide*. Just reading it will put on pounds.

$\mathcal{S}port$

NAPOLEON HAVING BEEN DEFEATED on the playing fields of Eton, games have been compulsory in British schools ever since. This helps to explain why London seethes with so much healthy, character-forming activity all the year round. With the probably crucial exceptions of American football and major league baseball, visiting sportsmen and fans can, depending on the season, watch or play just about anything. If they can't find a source of information about their particular passion in the following list, they should seek the advice of THE CENTRAL COUNCIL OF PHYSICAL RECREATION, 26 Park Crescent, W.1 (580-6822/9).

ATHLETICS

GOVERNING BODIES

AMATEUR ATHLETIC ASSOCIATION, 26 Park Crescent, W.1 (580-3498)

WOMEN'S AMATEUR ATHLETIC ASSOCIATION, 41 Hayward Court, Leverhurst Way, S.W.4 (622-8079)

The A.A.A. CHAMPIONSHIPS *take place at Crystal Palace in July. Affiliated clubs and associations hold meetings from April to October.*

ATHLETICS MEETINGS ARE HELD AT

CRYSTAL PALACE SPORTS CENTRE, Norwood, S.E.19 (778-0131)

WHITE CITY STADIUM, Shepherd's Bush, W.12 (743-5544)

HURLINGHAM PARK, Hurlingham Road, New King's Road, S.W.6 (736-5186)

Details of other London tracks and sports centers from the Parks Department, 2a Charing Cross Road, W.C.2 (836-5464).

AUTO RACING

ROYAL AUTOMOBILE CLUB, COMPETITIONS DEPARTMENT, 31 Belgrave Square, S.W.1 (235-8601)

BRITISH AUTOMOBILE RACING CLUB, SUTHERLAND HOUSE, 5 Argyll Street, W.1 (437-2533), will supply list of London clubs and race meetings.

BRITISH RACING & SPORTS CAR CLUB, EMPIRE HOUSE, Chiswick High Road, Chiswick, W.4 (995-0345)

AUTOMOBILE RACE MEETINGS HELD AT

CRYSTAL PALACE, S.E.19

BRANDS HATCH, Fawkham, Kent.

STOCK-CAR RACE MEETINGS HELD AT

WIMBLEDON STADIUM, Plough Lane, S.W.17 (946-5361)

HARRINGAY STADIUM, Green Lanes, N.4 (800-3474)

(SEE ALSO DRAG RACING)

BADMINTON

BADMINTON ASSOCIATION OF ENGLAND, 81a High Street, Bromley, Kent (460-5722) will supply details of badminton clubs in London.

All-England championships are held at the Empire Pool, Wembley, usually in March.

BASEBALL

BRITISH BASEBALL ASSOCIATION, 78 Connaught Road Barnet, Herts (440-2512).

Softball is played in Hyde Park (Knightsbridge end, near Wellington Barracks) every Sunday morning.

BASKETBALL

AMATEUR BASKETBALL ASSOCIATION, London Area Secretary, 19 Brewster Gardens, W.10 (969-0375)

National championships held at Crystal Palace.

Also extremely popular is the Harlem Globetrotters annual visit to Wembley.

BICYCLE POLO

BICYCLE ASSOCIATION OF GREAT BRITAIN, (inquiries: P. Wall, Llawnagol, 10 Priestley Drive, Tonbridge, Kent).

BILLIARDS & SNOOKER

BILLIARDS & SNOOKER CONTROL COUNCIL, 1/5 Salisbury Promenade, Green Lanes, Harringay, N.8 (802-6662)

A COUPLE OF BILLIARD AND SNOOKER HALLS:

THE CLARENCE BILLIARD SALOON, 201a High Holborn, W.C.1 (405-4929)

EMPIRE BILLIARDS AND TABLE TENNIS CLUB, 87-89 Shaftesbury Avenue, W.1 (437-7075)

BOATING

THE BEST PARKS WITH BOATING LAKES ARE:

THE SERPENTINE, Hyde Park, W.2 (row boats and sailing dinghies)

REGENT'S PARK, N.W.1

BATTERSEA PARK, Battersea, S.W.11

(SEE ALSO ROWING)

ROYAL YACHTING ASSOCIATION, 5 Buckingham Gate, S.W.1 (828-9296)

Lists RYA approved sailing schools.

BOWLING

BRITISH TEN PIN BOWLING ASSOCIATION, 19 Canterbury Avenue, Ilford, Essex (554-9137)

THERE ARE LANES OPEN AT:

PICCADILLY BOWL, Shaftesbury Avenue, W.1 (437-4200)

TOP RANK, Finchley Road, Golders Green, N.W.11 (455-9803)

WEMBLEY STADIUM BOWL, Empire Stadium, Wembley, (902-8560)

BOWLS

Bowling greens in Battersea Park and many other London parks.

BOXING

PROFESSIONAL BOXING

BRITISH BOXING BOARD OF CONTROL, Ramillies Buildings, Hills Place, W.1 (437-1475)

The main London arenas are: Empire Pool, Wembley; the Royal Albert Hall.

AMATEUR BOXING

AMATEUR BOXING ASSOCIATION, Clutha House, 10 Storeys Gate, S.W.1 (930-9207)

LONDON AMATEUR BOXING ASSOCIATION, 67 Central Buildings, 24 Southwark Street, S.E.1 (407-2194)

(Both will supply lists of boxing clubs and upcoming matches.)

The ABA championships are held in late Spring.
Boxing News for details of events.

CANOEING

BRITISH CANOE UNION, 26 Park Crescent, W.1 (580-4710)

Publish a guide to inland waterways.

CRICKET

Season runs from May to September.
LORD's, St. John's Wood Road, N.W.8 (289-1615)
Headquarters of the Marylebone Cricket Club, world governing body for cricket. Supplies information about the game.
Test match (international game) in June.

THE OVAL, Kennington Oval, S.E.11 (735-2424)
Test match in August.

Parks where cricket is played during the summer are: Wimbledon Common, Chiswick Park and Holland Park.

CROQUET

CROQUET ASSOCIATION, c/o Hurlingham Club, Putney Bridge, S.W.6 (736-8411) for information.

ROEHAMPTON CLUB, Roehampton Lane, S.W.15 (876-1621)

CYCLING

BRITISH CYCLING FEDERATION, 26 Park Crescent, W.1 (636-4602)

Information on various events, including road and track racing.

BRITISH CYCLING BUREAU, Greater London House, Hampstead Road, N.W.1 (387-0116). Will supply unusual and interesting cycling routes.

SOME LONDON TRACKS

CRYSTAL PALACE PARK, S.E.19 (details from B.C.F.)

PADDINGTON TRACK, Randolph Avenue, W.9 (624-1688) *Club racing every Tuesday.*

HERNE HILL STADIUM, Burbage Road, S.E. 24. Controlled by G.L.C. Parks Department (836-5464)

INDOOR EVENTS

Best are the professional, spectacular six-day indoor events staged at Wembley every September, the Skol International Six-Day Meeting.

BICYCLE RENTAL

SAVILLE'S CYCLE STORES, 97 Battersea Rise, S.W.11 (228-4279)

DARTS

DARTS ASSOCIATION OF GREAT BRITAIN (inquiries: Mr. J. Ross, 197 Fulwell Avenue, Clayhall, Ilford, Essex. (550-5171)

Traditional and highly skillful pub game.

DRAG RACING

BRITISH DRAG RACING & HOT ROD ASSOCIATION, 48 Whitehorse Lane, S.E.25 (653-5576)

Organizes events at various London airports.

(SEE ALSO AUTO RACING)

FENCING

AMATEUR FENCING ASSOCIATION, 83 Perham Road, W.14 (385-7442)

Further details from the Central Council of Physical Recreation.

FIELD HOCKEY

HOCKEY ASSOCIATION, 26 Park Crescent, W.1 (580-4840)

ALL ENGLAND WOMEN'S HOCKEY ASSOCIATION, 45 Doughty Street, W.C.1 (405-7514)

Details of clubs and dates of matches.

FISHING

LONDON ANGLERS' ASSOCIATION, 32 Stroud Green Road, N.4 (263-0196)

Anyone can fish in the Thames below Staines free of charge. It is also possible to fish in some of the lakes of the Royal and GLC parks (for the Royal parks, apply to the Parks Superintendent for a permit).

FLYING

BRITISH LIGHT AVIATION CENTRE, 75 Victoria Street, S.W.1 (222-6861)
Details of flying clubs, advice and information.

LONDON SCHOOL OF FLYING, Elstree Aerodrome, Boreham Wood, Herts (953-4411)

Flying training. Aircraft for hire.

FOX HUNTING

MASTER OF THE FOXHOUNDS ASSOCIATION, 137 Victoria Street, S.W.1 (799-7584)

THE ENFIELD CHASE, one of the nearest hunts to London. (Essendon 424)

GLIDING

BRITISH GLIDING ASSOCIATION, 75 Victoria Street, S.W.1 (799-7548)

Details of local gliding clubs.

GO-KART RACING

ROYAL AUTOMOBILE CLUB, Motor Sports Division, 31 Belgrave Square, S.W.1 (235-8601). For stock-car and go-kart racing information.

GOLF

PROFESSIONAL GOLFERS ASSOCIATION, Kennington Oval, S.E. 1 (735-8803)

GOLF FOUNDATION, LONDON SCOTTISH GOLF CLUB, Windmill Enclosure, Wimbledon Common, S.W.19 (789-7517)

Both will supply information.·

There are good public golf courses at Beckenham and Richmond Park as well as many private clubs with temporary membership facilities (try Hampstead [455-0203] or Dulwich [693-3961]).

GREYHOUND RACING

NATIONAL GREYHOUND RACING SOCIETY OF GREAT BRITAIN

LTD., St. Martin's House, 140 Tottenham Court Road, W.1
(387-0705)

SOME LONDON TRACKS

WEMBLEY EMPIRE STADIUM, Wembley, Middlesex (902-1234)
Monday and Friday 7:45 pm.

WHITE CITY STADIUM, Wood Lane, W.12 (743-5544)
Thursday and Saturday 7:45 pm.

WIMBLEDON STADIUM, Plough Lane, S.W.17 (946-5361)
Monday, Wednesday and Friday 7:45 pm.

GYMNASTICS

BRITISH AMATEUR GYMNASTICS ASSOCIATION, 26 Park Crescent, W.1 (580-4349)

HORSE RACING

JOCKEY CLUB & NATIONAL HUNT COMMITTEE, 42 Portman
Square, W.1 (486-4921)

RACE COURSES WITHIN EASY REACH OF LONDON:

ALEXANDRA PARK, Wood Green, N.22.

ASCOT, Berkshire.

EPSOM, Surrey.

KEMPTON PARK, Sunbury on Thames.

LINGFIELD PARK, Surrey.

SANDOWN PARK, Esher, Surrey.

WINDSOR PARK, Berkshire.

*Flat racing is from March to November; steeplechasing and
hurdle racing from August to June.*

ICE HOCKEY

BRITISH ICE HOCKEY ASSOCIATION, Empire House, 175 Piccadilly, W.1 (493-9791)

ICE SKATING

NATIONAL SKATING ASSOCIATION OF GREAT BRITAIN, Charterhouse, Charterhouse Square, E.C.1 (253-3824/5) for information.

THE MAJOR ICE SKATING RINKS ARE:

QUEEN'S ICE CLUB, Queensway, W.2 (229-0172)

THE SILVER BLADES, 386 Streatham High Road, S.W.16 (769-7861)

RICHMOND ICE RINK, Clevedon Road, East Twickenham. (892-3646)

JUDO

BRITISH JUDO ASSOCIATION, 26 Park Crescent, W.1 (580-7585)

Details of London clubs and championship events.

KARATE

BRITISH KARATE CONTROL COMMISSION, 26 Park Crescent, W.1 (580-6822)

LACROSSE

ENGLISH LACROSSE UNION, 3 Chessington Avenue, Bexleyheath. (Erith 36067)

LONDON AREA

SOUTH OF ENGLAND MEN'S LACROSSE ASSOCIATION, 282 Cassiobury Drive, Watford, Herts. (92-20293)

ALL-ENGLAND WOMEN'S LACROSSE ASSOCIATION, 26 Park Crescent, W.1 (636-1123)

MOTORCYCLE RACING

AUTO-CYCLE UNION, 31 Belgrave Square, S.W.1 (235-7636) for information on motorcycle racing.

NEW CROSS STADIUM, Hornshay Street, S.E.15 (639-0213)

WALTHAMSTOW STADIUM, Chingford Road, E.4 (527-2252)

(SEE ALSO UNDER SPEEDWAY)

NETBALL

ALL ENGLAND NETBALL ASSOCIATION, 26 Park Crescent, W.1 (580-3459)

PARACHUTING

BRITISH PARACHUTE ASSOCIATION, Artillery Mansions, 75 Victoria Street, S.W.1 (799-3760)

POLO

THE HURLINGHAM POLO ASSOCIATION, 2-4 Idle Lane, E.C.3 (626-4545) is the governing body and will supply details of clubs, matches, etc.

RAMBLING

RAMBLERS' ASSOCIATION, 124 Finchley Road, N.W.3 (435-7181)

RIDING

BRITISH HORSE SOCIETY, National Equestrian Centre, Stoneleigh, Kenilworth, Warwickshire (0203-27192) for general information.

THE GREATER LONDON HORSEMAN'S ASSOCIATION, 74 High Street, Teddington, Middlesex, will supply advice on riding in London.

For a stately canter along Rotten Row try one of these stables:

LILO BLUM, 32 Grosvenor Crescent Mews, S.W.1 (235-6846)

KNIGHTSBRIDGE RIDING SCHOOL, 11 Elvaston Mews, S.W.7 (584-8474)

For a good old gallop on Wimbledon Common or Richmond Park:

RIDGEWAY SCHOOL OF EQUITATION, 93 Ridgeway, Wimbledon, S.W.19 (946-7400)

(SEE ALSO UNDER SHOW JUMPING)

ROLLER SKATING

ALEXANDRA PALACE ROLLER RINK, Wood Green, N.22 (883-9711).

ROWING

AMATEUR ROWING ASSOCIATION, 160 Great Portland Street, W.1 (580-0854)

WOMEN'S AMATEUR ROWING ASSOCIATION, 20 Wensleydale Road, Hampton (979-3808)

The rowing season runs from March to September. The most notable events are the Oxford & Cambridge Boat Race, rowed between Putney and Mortlake in March, and the Henley Royal Regatta at Henley in June/July.
(SEE ALSO BOATING)

RUGBY

RUGBY FOOTBALL UNION, Whitton Road, Twickenham, Middlesex.

Rugby headquarters and stadium for many of the important matches. *Season is from September to April.*

SOME OF THE MAIN CLUBS

HARLEQUINS, Stoop Memorial Ground, Craneford Way, Twickenham (892-3080)

SARACENS, Bramley Sports Ground, Green Road, Chase Side, Southgate, N.14 (449-3770)

WASPS, Repton Avenue (off Eton Avenue) Sudbury (902-4220)

LONDON IRISH, The Avenue (off Thames Street) Sunbury-on-Thames (768-3034)

LONDON SCOTTISH, Athletic Ground, Kew Foot Road, Richmond (546-4801)

LONDON WELSH, Old Deer Park, Kew Road, Richmond (940-2520)

SCUBA DIVING

BRITISH SUB-AQUA CLUB, 160 Great Portland Street, W.1 (636-5667) for details of local branches.

SHOOTING

THE NATIONAL SMALL-BORE RIFLE ASSOCIATION, Codrington House, 113 Southwark Street, S.E.1 (928-3262)

THE NATIONAL RIFLE ASSOCIATION, Bisley Camp, Brookwood, Woking, Surrey (048-67-2213)

CLAY PIGEON SHOOTING ASSOCIATION, Eley Estate, Angel Road, N.18 (807-7528)

All three organizations will provide information, details of clubs, etc.

SHOW JUMPING

BRITISH SHOW JUMPING ASSOCIATION, National Equestrian

Centre, Stoneleigh, Kenilworth, Warwickshire (Coventry 20783).

THE TWO MAJOR LONDON EVENTS ARE

ROYAL INTERNATIONAL HORSE SHOW, White City Stadium, July

HORSE OF THE YEAR SHOW, Wembley, October.

The B.S.J.A. will supply details of other show-jumping events.

SKIING

NATIONAL SKI FEDERATION OF GREAT BRITAIN, 118 Eaton Square, S.W.1 (236-8228).

Information also from the Central Council of Physical Recreation.

ARTIFICIAL SKI SLOPES AVAILABLE AT

CRYSTAL PALACE NATIONAL RECREATION CENTER, Norwood, S.E.19 (778-0131).

SIMPSON (PICCADILLY) LIMITED, Philbeach Hall, Philbeach Gardens, S.W.5.

LILLYWHITES DRY SKI SCHOOL, Piccadilly Circus, S.W.1.

SOCCER

FOOTBALL ASSOCIATION, 22 Lancaster Gate, W.2.

LONDON FOOTBALL ASSOCIATION, Association House, 88 Lewisham High Street, S.E.13 (852-4777).

Soccer season is from August to April. Normal kick-off times, 3 pm. Saturday, 7:30 pm evening matches.

The F.A. Cup Final is held at the Empire Stadium, Wembley, in May. The League Cup Final is held in February.

THE FOLLOWING ARE THE MAIN PROFESSIONAL CLUBS IN LONDON

ARSENAL: Arsenal Stadium, Highbury, N.5 (226-3312).

CHELSEA: Stamford Bridge, Fulham Road, S.W.6 (385-5545).

CRYSTAL PALACE: Selhurst Park, Whitehouse Lane, Croydon, S.E.25 (653-2223).

FULHAM: Craven Cottage, Putney Bridge, S.W.6 (736-7035).

TOTTENHAM HOTSPURS: 748 High Road, Tottenham, N.17 (808-1020).

WEST HAM UNITED: Boleyn Ground, Green Street, E.13 (472-0704).

SPEEDWAY

SPEEDWAY CONTROL BOARD, 31 Belgrave Square, S.W.1 (235-8601).

RACING HELD AT

HACKNEY STADIUM, Waterden Road, E.15 (985-9822).

WEST HAM STADIUM, Custom House, E.16 (476-2441).

WIMBLEDON STADIUM, Plough Lane, S.W.17 (946-5361).

(See Daily Press for details)

SQUASH RACKETS

THE SQUASH RACKETS ASSOCIATION, 26 Park Crescent, W.1 (636-6901) for list of clubs and courts.

THERE ARE PUBLIC COURTS AT

DOLPHIN SQUARE, Grosvenor Road, S.W.1 (834-3800).

SWISS COTTAGE CIVIC CENTRE, 88 Avenue Road, N.W.3 (586-0061).

CRYSTAL PALACE SPORTS CENTRE, S.E.19 (778-0131).

STOCK CAR RACING

ROYAL AUTOMOBILE CLUB, Competitions Department, 31 Belgrave Square, S.W.1 (235-8601).

(SEE ALSO AUTO RACING)

SWIMMING

AMATEUR SWIMMING ASSOCIATION, Acorn House, Gray's Inn Road, W.C.1 (278-6751).

SOME INDOOR BATHS

OASIS BATHS, Holborn, W.C.2 (836-9555).

CRYSTAL PALACE SPORTS CENTRE, S.E.19 (778-0131).

SWISS COTTAGE CIVIC CENTRE, 88 Avenue Road, N.W.3 (586-0061).

CHELSEA BATHS, 36 Chelsea Manor Street, S.W.3 (352-6958).

SWIMMING OUTDOORS

SERPENTINE, Hyde Park, W.2 (435-2366).

HAMPSTEAD PONDS, N.W.3.

PARLIAMENT HILL LIDO, N.W.5 (485-3873).

TABLE TENNIS

ENGLISH TABLE TENNIS ASSOCIATION, 26 Park Crescent, W.1 (580-6312) for list of clubs, etc.

TENNIS

LAWN TENNIS ASSOCIATION, Baron's Court, West Kensington, W.14 (385-2366) is the governing body and will supply information.

ALL ENGLAND LAWN TENNIS & CROQUET CLUB, Church Road, Wimbledon, S.W.19 (946-2244) is where the famous Wimbledon Championships are staged in June/July each year.

QUEEN'S CLUB, Palliser Road, W.14 (385-3421) holds the National Covered Court Championship, usually in October.

There are public tennis courts in many London parks and also many clubs in and around London.

WATER· POLO

Amateur Swimming Association, Acorn House, Gray's Inn Road, W.C.1 (278-6751).

WEIGHT LIFTING

British Amateur Weight Lifters Association, Hon. Secretary—Mr. W. W. R. Holland, 3 Iffley Turn, Oxford, (tel: 0865-78319).

WRESTLING

British Amateur Wrestling Association, 60 Calabria Road, N.5 (226-3931) for list of London clubs.

Professional Wrestling (see daily press)

Theater

AMERICAN PRODUCERS are now finding it cheaper to mount a production in London and take it to New York only when they're sure they've got a hit. So get a jump on Clive Barnes. See the best of next year's Broadway season in London for a quarter of the price. The daily press will list what's running. And if you're interested in experimental drama and the avant garde, check on current productions at the following theaters and clubs:

ROYAL COURT, Sloane Square, S.W.1 (730-5174).

MERMAID, Puddle Dock, Upper Thames Street, E.C.4 (248-7656).

THE ROUNDHOUSE, Chalk Farm Road, N.W.1 (267-2564).

SHAW THEATRE, Euston Road, N.W.1 (388-1394).

REGENT'S PARK OPEN AIR THEATRE, Inner Circle, Regent's Park, N.W.1 (935-3696).

JEANETTE COCHRANE THEATRE, Southampton Row, W.C.1 (242-7040).

THE GREENWICH THEATRE, Crooms Hill, S.E.10 (858-7755).

LAMB & FLAG, Rose Street, off Garrick Street, W.C.2 (836-4108) (lunchtime plays).

THE NATIONAL YOUTH THEATRE, 81 Eccleston Square, S.W.1 (834-1085). Performances at the Shaw Theatre, 100 Euston Road, N.W.1.

THE YOUNG VIC, The Cut, Waterloo, S.E.1 (928-7616).

THEATER CLUBS

THEATRE UPSTAIRS, Royal Court Theatre, Sloane Square, S.W.1 (730-5174).

PLAYERS, Villiers Street, W.C.2 (839-5086).

MOUNTVIEW THEATRE CLUB, 104 Crouch Hill, N.8 (340-5885).

TOWER THEATRE, Canonbury Tower, Canonbury Place, N.1 (226-5111).

THE ARTS THEATRE CLUB, 6-7 Great Newport Street, W.C.2 (836-3334).

OPEN SPACE, 32 Tottenham Court Road, W.1 (580-4970).

HAMPSTEAD THEATRE CLUB, Swiss Cottage Centre, N.W.3 (722-9301).

KINGS HEAD THEATRE CLUB, 115 Upper Street, N.1 (226-1916). London's first pub/theater.

PUPPET THEATER

THE LITTLE ANGEL MARIONETTE THEATRE, 14 Dagmar Passage, N.1 (226-1787).
Shows every Saturday and Sunday.

Tourist/Travel Services

LONDON TOURIST BOARD

4 Grosvenor Gardens, S.W.1 (730-0791).
Open Monday to Friday 9:15 am to 5:30 pm. General inquiries, including accommodation.

ALSO INFORMATION BUREAUS AT:

Victoria Railway Station (opposite platform 9), *daily 7:30 am to 11 pm.*
BOAC Air Terminal, S.W.1. Arrivals Hall, *daily 8 am to 4 pm.*

BRITISH TRAVEL AUTHORITY

64 St. James's Street, S.W.1 (629-9191).
Open Monday to Friday 9 am to 6 pm, Saturday 9 am to 12:30 pm.

CITY OF LONDON INFORMATION CENTRE

St. Paul's Churchyard, E.C.4 (606-3030 extension 236).
Open Monday to Friday 9:30 am to 5 pm.
Saturday 9:30 am to 12:30 pm.

Advice and information dealing exclusively with the City.

DAILY TELEGRAPH INFORMATION SERVICE
(353-4242).

GREATER LONDON INFORMATION

County Hall, S.E.1 (633-3000).
Open Monday to Friday 9 am to 6 pm.

General inquiries on the Greater London Council and London borough councils.

TELETOURIST (246-8041). Recorded list of daily events in London.

BUS & UNDERGROUND

LONDON TRANSPORT, 55 Broadway, S.W.1 (222-1234). *24-hour service.*

Branches at following underground stations: Oxford Circus, Piccadilly, King's Cross, Euston, Victoria, St. James's Park.

(LONG-DISTANCE) BUSES

VICTORIA COACH STATION, 164 Buckingham Palace Road, S.W.1 (730-0202).

KING'S CROSS COACH STATION, Caledonia Street, N.1 (837-7373).

CAR RENTALS

HERTZ, 243 Knightsbridge, S.W.7 (581-2751).

AVIS, 68 North Row, W.1 (629-7811).

GUIDEBOOKS

Companion Guide to London; David Piper; Fontana, 50p.

Using London; Royds, Tuft and Manley; Penguin, 35p.

Alternative London; Saunders and Cucksey; Saunders, 30p.

GUIDES

GUILD OF GUIDE LECTURERS. Booking Bureau: 930-7687 (April to October).

ROAD

AUTOMOBILE ASSOCIATION (A.A.), Leicester Square, W.C.2 (954-7373).

ROYAL AUTOMOBILE CLUB (R.A.C.), 89 Pall Mall, S.W.1 (930-2345).

RAIL

BRITISH RAIL TRAVEL CENTRE, Lower Regent Street, S.W.1 (personal callers only).

BRITISH RAIL INFORMATION SERVICE (387-7070).

EASTERN REGION—King's Cross Station (837-3355). Liverpool Street & Fenchurch Street Station (283-7171).

LONDON MIDLAND REGION—Euston and St. Pancras Stations (387-7070).

SOUTHERN REGION—Charing Cross, London Bridge, Victoria & Waterloo Stations (928-5100).

CONTINENTAL & CHANNEL ISLAND INQUIRIES—834-2345.

CONTINENTAL CAR FERRY CENTRE—730-3440.

WESTERN REGION—Paddington Station (262-6767).

SIGHTSEEING

BY BOAT

THAMES TRIPS—to the Tower, Greenwich, Hampton Court. *Daily 10 am to 7 pm from Charing Cross Pier* (839-5320), Westminster Pier (930-2074); and Tower Pier (709-9855).

FOR BOAT RENTALS AND SPECIAL TRIPS, try:

THAMES LAUNCHES & CRUISES LTD. (892-9041).

THAMES PLEASURE CRAFT LTD. (709-9697).

A. T. WOOD LAUNCHES LTD. (481-2711).

THAMES MOTOR BOAT CO. (734-7431).

CATAMARAN CRUISES LTD. (987-1185).

DOCK TRIPS:

ROYAL DOCKS, Port of London Authority (709-2000).

CANAL TRIPS:

JASON'S TRIP (286-3428).

JENNY WREN (485-6210).

ZOO WATERBUS (286-6101).

BY ROAD

AMERICAN EXPRESS (930-4411).

THOMAS COOK (499-4000).

FRAMES (387-3488).

LONDON TRANSPORT TOURS (222-1234).

BY AIR

HELICOPTER TRIPS.
Saturdays from Westland London Heliport (228-7820).

TRAVEL AGENTS

AMERICAN EXPRESS, 6 Haymarket, S.W.1 (930-4411).
THOMAS COOK, 45 Berkeley Street, W.1 (499-4000).

Glossary

ANGLO	AMERICAN
banger	sausage
bed and breakfast	room plus breakfast
bent	dishonest
bespoke	hand tailored
bob	former shilling, now 5 new pence
bobby	policeman
booking	reservation
bonnet (car)	hood
boot (car)	trunk
caravan	trailer
chemist	drugstore
chips	french fries
cinema	movie theater
civvies	civilian dress
coach	long distance bus
counterfoil	receipt or copy
crisps	potato chips
demo	political demonstration
directory inquiries (phone)	information
dishy	good-looking (male or female)
engaged (phone)	busy
fag	cigarette
football	soccer/rugby
fortnight	two weeks
frankfurter	pork sausage, usually
full up	no more room
gateau	cake
ground floor	first or main floor
have a go	take a turn or try something
hire	rent

ANGLO	AMERICAN
hire purchase	installment plan
holiday	vacation
interval	intermission
ironmongers	hardware store
kiosk	booth
knickers	underpants (ladies)
L (red letter on vehicle)	learner driver
lift	elevator
liqueurs	cordials
loo, bog	toilet
lorry	truck
lower ground floor	basement
nappies	diapers
newsstall (bookstall)	newsstand
not to worry	never mind
off the peg	ready made
overtake	pass
pants	underpants (men)
pardon?	what did you say?
pavement	sidewalk
petrol	gasoline
pillar box	mail box
poof	fag or fairy
post	mail
pudding	dessert or sometimes a pudding
quid	pound (100 new pence)
queue	line of people
raver	enthusiastic trendy
rave-up	party
reel of cotton	spool of thread
ring up	phone
road	street
roundabout	traffic circle
salt beef	corned beef
subway	underground pedestrian passage
sweet	dessert
sweets	candy
taps	faucets

ANGLO	AMERICAN
telly	TV
tights	panty hose
tin	can
tobacconist	cigarette store
trousers	pants (men), slacks (women)
trendy	swinger
tube	subway
underground	subway
venue	location
vest	man's undershirt
waistcoat	man's vest
wardrobe	closet
W.C.	toilet
Zed	Z

Index

Trooping the Color, 143
Turret Bookship, 10, 128
Tyburn Gallows, 141

Urban planning, 8-9, 16-17, 19-20, 59, 67, 108-109
U.S. Embassy, 113

Vauxhall Bridge, 16
Victoria and Albert Museum, 50, 98, 159
Victoria Square, 74
Victorian Society, The, 120
Vincent Square, 71, 144, 147
Vintners Company, 144

Wallace Collection, 122
Wardrobe Place, 55
Water polo, 197
Waterman's Arms, 93, 175
Weightlifting, 197
Wellington Museum, 122-123
Westbourne Grove, 42, 134
Westbury Hotel, 102-103, 152, 166
Westminster, City of, 38, 50

Westminster, Palace of, 38, 70
  see also Parliament, Houses of
Westminster Abbey, 14, 50, 70, 71, 140, 145, 146
Westminster Bridge, 14, 16, 142
Westminster Cathedral, 71-72
Westminster Hall, 70
What's On, 157, 165
Wheeler's, 105-106, 179
White Tower, 105, 178
Whitechapel Art Gallery, 123
Whitehall, 68, 70, 147
Whitehall Palace, 15, 70, 120
Widow's Son, The, 94, 141, 175
Wilton Row, 88
Wilton's, 106, 178
Woburn Walk, 65, 120
World War I, 17, 33
World War II, 18-19, 32, 52, 54, 55, 58, 62, 94, 103, 145
Wren, Christopher, 16, 19, 47, 52, 53, 54, 55, 56, 57, 58, 59, 69, 120, 171
Wrestling, 197
Wyatt, S., 51

Zoo, The, 76, 172